How Viktor Orbán Plays To Win: The Resurgence of Central Europe

Thibaud Gibelin

Foreword by Rod Dreher

How Viktor Orbán Plays To Win:
The Resurgence of Central Europe

Thibaud Gibelin

Foreword by Rod Dreher

Academica Press
Washington~London

Library of Congress Cataloging-in-Publication Data
Names: Gibelin, Thibaud (author)
Title: How viktor orban plays to win : the resurgence of central Europe |
Gibelin, Thibaud
Description: Washington : Academica Press, 2025. | Includes references.
Identifiers: LCCN 2024945076 | ISBN 9781680533194 (hardcover) |
9781680533200 (e-book)

Contents

Exordium

"An extraordinary imagination animated this cold politician: he wouldn't have been what he was if the muse hadn't been there; reason fulfilled the poet's ideas. All these men with great lives are always a compound of two natures, for they must be capable of inspiration and action: one gives birth to the project, the other accomplishes it."

François-René de Chateaubriand, *Mémoires d'outre-tombe*

People walk on their land and under the stars, and only secondarily on asphalt and under streetlights. One's origins never disappear, tradition never dies out; we reconnect with both. These eclipses, after all, are as necessary as winters: the most thankless historical circumstances reveal invincible permanences.

Viktor Orbán has found himself the medium of a sensibility that was thought to have disappeared. In him, disparate traditions have regained an intelligible meaning; the sense of origins has found the blossoming of becoming. Just when history was supposed to come to an end, it resumed its course in a land of misfortune and in a dissident who rallied to the change of regime in 1989. Viktor Orbán represents more than he is. He draws his strength from a tradition that is opposed to and strengthened against contemporary nihilism. He is neither uptight nor cold-hearted, but brimming with optimism and the offensive spirit of a hussar. His political cavalcade continues under the rolling fire of liberal artillery, just as it began in the shadow of the Iron Curtain: on the front line.

Foreword

Rod Dreher

Hungary's Viktor Orbán is the longest continuously serving leader of a Western democracy, and easily the most controversial. It is not hard to understand why. As a nationalist and populist of the political right, Orbán's convictions and governing policies typically run counter to the liberal governing consensus in Europe and North America.

When most of Europe opened its borders to masses of third world refugees in 2015, Orbán said no. He didn't refuse because he has a hard heart. He did it because he understood well that most of these people were not actual refugees, but third world men looking for a permanent foothold in Europe. And he knew then, as he knows now, that the survival of distinct European nations depends on stopping the unregulated flow of migrants.

When elites throughout the West changed laws to permit same-sex marriage, and to allow for teaching children – in schools and in popular culture – about the so-called virtues of homosexuality and gender ideology, Orbán put his foot down. Not here in Hungary, he said. The traditional family is the basis of civilization. Childhood innocence should be protected.

When NATO carried out its proxy war with Russia, via Ukraine, Orbán refused to allow Hungary to get involved. They called him "Putin's lapdog." In fact, Orbán knew that Ukraine could not prevail against Russia, that the West had unwisely provoked the conflict, and that continuing the war would not only destroy Ukraine, but impoverish Europe, and possibly lead to a wider conflagration.

So, here's the standard portrait of Viktor Orban, as seen without question in the Western media: a right-wing bully, dictator, and bigot who is Putin's European cat's paw. They also claim that Orbán's Hungary is a semi-fascist state where freedom is under siege, and the independent media faces clampdown.

Funny, but that's not how it looks from Budapest, where I have lived for the past three years. And it's not how it looks to many first-time visitors from elsewhere in the West.

While Western European capitals are ridden with migrant crime and dirt, Budapest is safe and clean. A man in from Germany said to me that unlike back home, there is active and joyful street life in Budapest; in German cities, people have withdrawn over fears of violent crime. A visitor from Paris told me on an after-dinner stroll through downtown, "I feel like I'm back in Europe again."

Where children in the United States, the United Kingdom, and other countries that have promoted LGBTQ+ ideology are suffering from off-the-charts anxiety, the mental health of Hungarian children is comparatively stable. Perhaps owing to the Orbán government's generous policies encouraging childbearing, marriage rates in Hungary have doubled over the last ten years, even as they have mostly collapsed elsewhere in Europe.

And now, as the Russia-Ukraine war grinds on into its third gruesome year, with the Russian economy booming and most of the world having defied the West's calls for a crusade, the Hungarian leader's early warnings about the foolishness of Western meddling have been borne out by events.

In the late summer of 2024, Britain was rocked by anti-migrant rioting that spurred a sharply authoritarian response from UK authorities. Judges began sending Britons to jail for having posted disfavored memes and comments on social media. Even as mobs of Muslim men rampaged through city streets shouting, "*Allahu akbar*" and looking for lone, Union Jack-sporting white Englishmen to beat up, the government and the media raged against alleged right-wing hooligans for causing the trouble, and fumed about Elon Musk's X (formerly Twitter), which was the only place British people could actually see what was happening on their streets.

None of this happened in Hungary. The country is safe and calm because the Orbán government – unlike successive UK governments – listens to and respects the will of the electorate, which says no to migration. And unlike in Britain, the birthplace of liberal democracy, no Hungarian has ever been thrown in jail for complaining about migrants on social media.

Plainly, Viktor Orbán is doing something right. His enemies in other countries can't admit it, because doing so raises an obvious question: *why are they failing?*

In my time in Hungary, I have encouraged American conservative leaders to visit Hungary and learn from Orbán's strategies. In *How Viktor Orbán Plays To Win*, Thibaud Gibelin, a French writer who has also been living in Hungary and observing Orbán's strategy up close, explains that the Hungarian prime minister is a visionary whose understanding of how the contemporary world works is based on a way of seeing it in a fundamentally different way from the globalist politicians and theorists of the postwar transatlantic establishment.

Orbán believes that the world is facing a realignment the likes of which hasn't been seen in five centuries. He believes that the survival of Western peoples, and their thriving, depends on the strength of individual nations. That, in turn, requires strong families, and cohesive communities made up of people who believe in their ancestral faith and in the goodness of their own people and cultural traditions.

More prosaically, Orbán understands that culture and politics are entwined in ways that most Western conservatives, as inheritors of the liberal tradition, do not see. In most liberal democracies, left-wingers have marched successfully through all the institutions of cultural formation – especially schools, universities, and the media – and use their institutional power to marginalize conservatives and to turn the younger generations into loyal servants of progressive causes and left-wing power-holders.

What's more, Viktor Orbán is willing to fight, and fight hard. Perhaps it's because he got his start in politics as a young David facing down the communist Goliath. Perhaps it's because as the leader of a small central European country that has had to wage war for its very existence for a thousand years, Orbán cannot afford to see the world in sentimental liberal abstractions. His enemies in Washington, Brussels, and other Western capitals regard Orbán as a Magyar barbarian. In fact, he is the best political response the right has to the globalist, post-Christian genteel barbarism that has overtaken the ruling class throughout the West.

The United States is a mammoth country compared to Hungary, but the best parts of the American soul and way of life are under sustained attack by a hydra-headed enemy that many conventional American conservatives can scarcely identify. Viktor Orbán sees the foe clearly, and he has all his political life. He has a plan for victory. And he knows what time it is.

In these pages, Thibaud Gibelin tells the tale. This is not a story Americans will hear from their media or from establishment historians. But it is a tale they must hear, take to heart, and take to the political and cultural battlefield -- while there is still time.

Rod Dreher
Budapest, August 2024

Introduction

The European Union facing a repressed Europe

One question hangs over the European continent: what is the future of its unity? It influences the future of every nation and the daily lives of hundreds of millions of citizens. For some, it remains an idea to be supported or rejected, but it is also an ongoing historical conditioning that we must accept in order to curb. Those who detach themselves from it submit to it, while those who attach themselves to it retain a chance to see their views prevail. The European Union (EU) is political insofar as what goes beyond it (national future, morals, education, health, ecology, security, etc.) is also decided by it. Never has its role seemed more decisive, and at the same time its software more exhausted.

In Brussels and in European chancelleries, opposition is often confined to discrete pugilistic brawls, which sometimes spill over onto the airwaves and the stage. The media's polemical, publicity-driven approach to public debate inevitably impoverishes civil discourse. It imposes the false idea of a single alternative: the dismantling of the European Union on the one hand, and the establishment of a United States of Europe on the other. However crude, this simplification teaches us two things: there are several competing visions of Europe, and we do not know what shape the European Union will take in the decades to come.

The current dispute arises from a war of ideas. Liberal democracy has recently imposed itself on the countries of the continent. Broadly speaking, the European Union is based on two principles: democracy and liberalism. One is based on the sovereignty of the people, the other on the authority of law. Today, these two principles diverge, to the extent that half of the European Union is at war with the other. The right of peoples to self-determination clashes with the unlimited rights of the individual; the claims of liquid society clash with the tenants of historical continuity; national democracies sometimes retain their sovereignty and sometimes give short shrift to the rules that frame them. Should we agree with Jean-Claude Juncker that "there is no democracy outside the European treaties?"[1] That the European nations were merely the interminable prologue to a federal state? Or that European integration was just another failed attempt to unify the continent?

More than ever, Europe resides in its nations. Today's political fragmentation is at odds with the degree of integration of the single market, as if economic promiscuity were creating new frictions. The United Kingdom has already left the Union. Liberal utilitarianism is aggravating the disaffiliation of countries and individuals alike. Selfishness is at work everywhere, nowhere more so than in the economic arena. The reality of a European *oikos* is withering away, while the oxymoronic "economic community," stripped of the halo of civilization that justified it in the first place, confesses its fatal contradiction.

Let us recall where the European Union came from to understand why its de facto political stature is so uncertain. Its manifest destiny lies in the slim "Schuman Declaration" of May 9, 1950, which urged European countries to "make concrete achievements, first creating a de facto solidarity." The European adventure began modestly, as a union of producers of steel and coal – a meagre but important share of the civilizational capital of a continent admired as the beacon of the world forty years earlier. With the Treaty of Rome (1958), however, the establishment of the European Economic Community (EEC) indicated that the only quality retained to forge the unitary framework of six countries of the Christian West was that of homo economicus.

Since Philippe de Villiers's well-documented essay,[2] we know that the intentions of the "Fathers of Europe" were neither good nor innocent. These peaceful pioneers in the ruins of the Old Continent advocated "the establishment of an economic community and the leavening of a wider and deeper community between countries long opposed by bloody divisions." However "broader and deeper" the community may have become, it has been reduced to economics. Worse still, it has reduced Europe to it. Building the economy as providence is no apotheosis; it happened because

---

[1] Interview with *Le Figaro*, January 28, 2015.
[2] Philippe de Villiers, *J'ai tiré sur le fil du mensonge et tout est venu*, Fayard, 2019.

nothing could contain its ascendancy in a Europe demoralized by the de facto civil war of 1914-1945. The continent was crushed before it was swindled. The bewilderment of Europe's peoples and the weakness of its nations were revealed in this abandonment to an apolitical, accounting logic, endowed with an elementary liberal catechism teaching that a big market is better than a small one, and that the decline of countries prepares the way for them to be taken over at the supranational level: the world is only flat because of the debasement of peoples.

The blame lies not so much with the founders of European integration as with their docile successors, who failed to nurture an imperfect graft of all that is noble about Europe. More seriously, the neoliberal turn taken by the EEC under the Delors Commission (1985-1995) refocused the European project on the single market and generalized competition. This orientation undoubtedly runs counter to the efforts initiated by Robert Schuman, accompanied by Charles de Gaulle and Konrad Adenauer. At the time, the triumph of the Anglo-Saxon model in the face of the collapse of socialism was likely to inspire emulation. Some believed that the end of history had arrived, and that Europe was anticipating the establishment of a peaceful world market. These illusions have been disavowed, but the old guard of decision-makers still largely in power remains imbued with them.

The EEC became the European Union with the adoption of the Maastricht Treaty in 1992. It still suffers from enormous handicaps in asserting itself as a political community, as its DNA demands an impossible neutrality. Defining otherness, distinguishing friend from foe, delimiting borders, territorializing power, subordinating growth to other objectives: these are all phobias that will blight the Union's future.

In the irony of history, which confers a belated radiance on dead ideas, as it does on stars, liberal Europe gave itself an "empire in spite of itself." Between 2004 and 2013, eleven countries of former socialist Europe and two islands in the Mediterranean joined, with further expansion in the works. The limits of the current European project are perceived with particular acuity by the nations of Central Europe, precisely because they did not initiate it.

*

The *"Trente glorieuses"* – the thirty prosperous years following World War II in Western Europe, preceded what we might call the *"Trente fangeuses"* ("thirty muddy years"), which witnesses the triumph of vulgar materialism. They also coincided with East Europeans suffering and dying under Soviet repression. In 1956, "for Hungary and for Europe," in the words of the telex sent to the world by the head of Hungary's press agency, this included the Hungarian Revolution. In 1968, Czechoslovakian leader Alexander Dubček's efforts to reform socialism ended in the intervention of Warsaw Pact armies. The burning of Jan Palash, Jan Zajic, and Evzen Plocek shines in the twilight of the Prague Spring. These martyrs repeated the gesture of the Pole Ryszard Siwiec, whose suicide struck 100,000 people gathered at the Stadion Dziesięciolecia as part of a propaganda event, a sacrifice that echoed the struggle of the "accursed soldiers," including Josef Francziak, a hero of the Polish resistance assassinated in 1963. Similar figures include the "Forest Brothers" in the Baltic States and the peasant rebels against collectivization entrenched in Romania. It is also the rebellious soul of a free people, exemplified in the great Polish social movement, Solidarność.

These struggles bear witness to the importance of spiritual resources. May these two forces go hand in hand, and may they never ignore each other: may Antigone stand before Creon if she is not at his side. The articulation of these two forces – law and faith, reason and spirit, lucidity and inspiration – largely determines the history of peoples. Particularly in the countries of Central Europe, distrust of the righteousness of foreign power is fundamental. This periphery of present-day Europe, hardened by the ordeal, is as firmly rooted as ever in the heart of our civilization.

This assertion deserves a brief illustration. Respect for the law is a cardinal virtue that the authorities in Brussels like to claim, especially when they condemn Central European countries for alleged "breaches of the rule of law," often backing up their criticism with financial threats. Yet the law is no less respected in Budapest than it is in Brussels. It simply draws on deeper sources than "protecting the individual from coercion."[3]

---

[3] In the words of Fareed Zakaria. In a contribution entitled "The Rise of Illiberal Democracy," published in *Foreign Affairs* in 1997, the Indian-American political scientist

In the Hungarian example, law is one authority among others in the service of the common good, so that Hungary may be and remain itself. A Hungarian will die for his nation, and *ipso facto* for the law that exercises authority within it. But no Westerner would die for the "rule of law." In these troubled times, this difference is immense.

*

The collapse of the Eastern bloc was a contradiction in terms in European history, as the people's victory over communism was seen as a plebiscite in favor of the Western model. History was thought to have come to an end, just as people were proving that it could be resurrected. The misunderstanding is colossal: Western Europe's subjection to the Atlantic bloc was sanctioned by an apparent triumph. It gave liberal Europe the feeling of having won, alongside the United States, while the laurels went to the Slavs, Baltic peoples, and Magyars to the east of the Iron Curtain, who exhausted communism by stubbornly rejecting its legitimacy. The tamed masses of the West gave the dominant ideology the endurance of victory, while it was the newly liberated peoples of the East who scuttled socialism.

It was not a question of preferring one system or the other, but of rejecting one or the other once one was subjected to it. The Europeans of the time decided at their own pace, as allowed by circumstances. It is up to today's Europeans to decide what to do with this heritage, which belongs fully to them as it weighs on their shoulders.

Nevertheless, the East-West divide in the EU is not simply a legacy of the Cold War. To believe so would be to endow communism with a conservative virtue it never had. Post-war regimes diminished Central European countries culturally, politically, and economically. Socialism worked towards the advent of a materialist, post-national era just as much as liberalism. This fundamental convergence between the two ideologies explains East Germans' ingenuous fascination with capitalist abundance, as portrayed in the film *Good Bye, Lenin!* (2003). State materialism existed elsewhere, and it did not require collectivism. In addition, socialism and

---

defends the precedence of liberalism over democracy, on the grounds that it is the former that enables the latter.

liberalism were competitors on both sides of the Iron Curtain, and on the whole, respected each other. This helps to explain the brutal metamorphoses of societies "liberated" from Soviet pressure over the past thirty years.

*

There is indeed a major Europe on the continent: the Carolingian core, with its high concentration of population, wealth, power, and skill. This megalopolis, extending from the mouth of the Rhine to the highest of the Alps and from Paris to Frankfurt, has remained more or less the heart of the continent since the fall of the Roman Empire. There is also a Europe Minor, on the eastern flank of core Western Europe. But is Western Europe today living up to its birthright? Do the countless setbacks of recent years not indicate that we have reached the end of a long-standing impasse? If Carolingian Europe remains the continent's center of gravity, it does so at the risk of sinking it: it lacks a fulcrum. It can find it in the Europe of Visegrád, its alter ego, its guilty conscience, and its forerunner in the new century.

The twists and turns of an encrypted Europe

The Visegrád Group (V4) comprises four European Union countries: Hungary, Poland, the Czech Republic, and Slovakia. The group has a population of 64 million over an area of 530,000 km,^{2} the size of metropolitan France, on the eastern flank of the Germanic world, and on the borders of the former Soviet Union.

In 1335, the kings of Bohemia, Hungary, and Poland joined forces at Visegrád, a fortress overlooking the Danube north of Buda, to counter the encroachments of their powerful neighbor, Austria. This was the historical reference point when, on February 15, 1991, a cooperation treaty was signed between these same three countries to prepare for their entry into the European Union. The concerted dissolution of Czechoslovakia on December 31, 1992, led to the reshaping of the V3 into the V4.

We need to delve into the long history of these countries to understand what Viktor Orbán is all about. To make sense of the evolution of the Visegrád group – particularly its aptitude for international cooperation – Poland and Hungary had been major Christian states for centuries. The

Czech Republic, formerly known as Bohemia-Moravia, was also a kingdom with important privileges, albeit within an earlier limited supranational state, the Holy Roman Empire. Slovakia formally emerged in European history in the twentieth century, when it ceased to be a Slavic province ruled by the Kingdom of Hungary. While these neighbors proved "fast adjustors" after 1989, they also share a history of domination by invading hegemonic powers.

*

For the V4 countries, the collapse of communism opened up an obvious and exhilarating prospect: a return to the European family, which they had joined a thousand years earlier and within which their nations had grown and prospered. No treaty, no legal strictures, no forced economic march – just a simple return to *themselves*. You might as well imagine a man returning home after a long prison sentence: he would not ask how the house has been fitted out or how the household chores are organized. He just wants to be with his family again. Such was the state of mind of these peoples when they applied for membership in the European Union.

But as we have already mentioned, liberalism, freed from socialist competition, has revived a revolutionary dynamic. This was boosted by the lightning conquest of new markets and the takeover of Eastern industries at the cost of unemployment for millions of workers, to rebuild a productive apparatus complementary to and dependent on Western capitalism.

Central Europe submitted to the law of the victor and put on a brave face on the liberal paradise imposed upon it. As long as the stupefaction of peoples dazed by communism was maintained, as long as the West's successes made its principles indisputable, as long as promises outweighed distress, the certainty that "there is no alternative" – as Margaret Thatcher put it with regard to liberal globalization – could remain.

This state of affairs has been evolving since the 2008 financial crisis, which launched an upheaval in Europe and around the world. The decline of liberalism began to take shape: the dogmas of Western Europe were shaken before they could be assimilated by the peoples of Central Europe. Since then, every failure of the system has called for a response forged *hic et nunc* by nations in an uncertain world. The global crisis spawned by the Covid-19 pandemic marked a significant milestone along the road travelled. The effectiveness of Central European countries in the face of the pandemic bears witness to this fact: the political impasse lies not in the nations themselves, but in the ideology that undermines them.

*

Some men play a catalytic role in history. They give an era its face. The insurrection of reality appears in Central Europe in the shape of Viktor Orbán. From dissidence to the communist system in the 1980s, to dissidence to the liberal model in the 2010s, the political trajectory of this extraordinary leader follows or anticipates the evolution of mentalities in Hungary and Central Europe. Viktor Orbán is already a page of history, but a living page whose reading not only offers us valuable insights into recent history, but also foreshadows of the twists and turns to come.

The continuing success of the Hungarian Prime Minister shows that he is neither isolated nor lost. In neighboring countries, too, national elites supported by their people aspire to a more nation-protecting Europe, preferring the immense heritage of the Christian centuries to the conditional pleasures of mass consumption. This wish may not be unanimous, but events from 2014 to 2024 prove it, starting with the rejection of Brussels's lax yet coercive migration policy: nothing could have happened if a spark of nobility had not survived.

*

I do not intend to reassure Western Europeans with the illusion that others will bail them out. The figure of the rustic Central European is not destined to take the same place in the imagination of many pessimists as the migrant occupies in that of "progressives." My aim is to help demonstrate two things: that it is politically possible to do well in the Europe of the 2020s, even within the imperfect framework of Brussels; and that a movement that transcends the EU and will outlive it is now emerging.

It would be wrong to judge the European Union solely by its setbacks, and indeed Central Europe has good reason to look back with pride on much of the past twenty years of EU institutions. At a time when the balance of power is first and foremost economic, when the means of power are inseparable from the capacity to finance it, Central Europe has grown considerably richer. The former Soviet satellites are leading the way in terms of all continental economic indicators: growth in industrial production, full employment, wage increases, balanced budgets, and so on.

European structural funds, of which the V4 is a net beneficiary, contribute to this upturn. But transfers from Central Europe to Western economies more than offset this expenditure. The distribution of roles between the winners and losers of European integration is far more complex than one might imagine. In addition to contributions to the EU budget, we will see which sectors of the economy and which segments of the population reap the benefits of the collective effort.

It is worth remembering that labor costs in the V4 countries are only 35% (in Poland) to 45% (in the Czech Republic) of the EU average. Even on a purchasing power parity basis, GDP per capita is 65% (in Hungary) to 80% (in the Czech Republic) of that of the EU15. This situation of inferiority is patiently endured by the tens of millions of workers who prefer austere remuneration to expatriation.

Since the destruction of the Austro-Hungarian empire over a century ago, this region has remained fragmented or oppressed under a foreign yoke. It has proceeded toward regaining its former stature thanks to the infrastructure linking the continent: the building of a European economy that is once again united does not run counter to the tradition of these countries. Finally, a unified continental perspective, achieved through twenty years of effort, deserves praise.

*

Economics and politics have their own laws. The Europe of Visegrád intends to subordinate the former to the latter. In the years or since their accession to the EU, new member states grown richer without really suffering from the vagaries of their supranational allegiance. But in the long term, the deployment of liberal logic implies the evolution of social structures and mentalities under the pressures of dominant financial pressures. Western countries preceded the V4 on this path, but the historical circumstances differ. The migration crisis in progress since 2014 finally made it possible to distinguish between the concessions a people can make and the resignations to which it cannot stoop. A red line has been drawn on this point: "No one can force us to accept foreign populations on our soil." But the minders in Brussels think differently.

The Visegrád group's rebuff may seem anecdotal at first. Refusing to welcome a few thousand migrants simply means missing an opportunity, if we agree with liberal elites that they are a precious resource. This controversy is shaking Europe because, under Viktor Orbán's prodding, Europe is rediscovering itself for what it once was: a framework for the flourishing of its constituent nations. Central Europe is awakening to the EU's dual personality: a haven in which to endure and a project to which to submit, the "Doctor Jekyll" of the continent's unitary face and the "Mister Hyde" of faceless cosmopolitanism.

In other words, a dominated Europe is becoming aware of a dominant Europe within it, and the balance of power is rapidly shifting: the prospect of a different policy is conceivable because it is desired by the continent's peoples as reflected by their elected governments. It is remarkable that the parties in power in Budapest, Bratislava, Prague, and (until very recently) Warsaw all belong to likeminded political formations. The Hungarian Fidesz Party has long been a member of the European People's Party (EPP). The Slovak SMER is a member of the Party of European Socialists (PES). The Czech ODS belongs to the European Conservatives and Reformists (ECR), as does the Polish PiS, in power between 2015 and 2023.

That the opposition is not limited to popular discontent, but involves a coalition of democratic states, is evidence of a de facto revolution in governance. This response is coordinated within the current framework of European institutions, proving that it is not entirely incapacitating. We have come a long way since 2010, when Viktor Orbán, armed only with a constitutional majority, regained power in a ruined and disoriented Hungary. In July 2018, the Hungarian leader, triumphantly re-elected, concluded his annual speech at Tusványos:[4] "Thirty years ago, Europe was

---

[4] Speech on July 28, 2018, Bálványos Summer University. This event has been held annually in Transylvania since the fall of communism and includes an address by Viktor

our future, today we are Europe's future."

Faced with the return of history, the European Union is paradoxically becoming a sounding board for the major issues of our century, and a forum for cooperating nations, rather than a superstate governing in "ever closer union." The new force at work is that part of Europe is being reborn. The future prospects of the alternative now being created are as unknown as they are contested. They could be immense, for Europe has many rival examples in its history and enormous resources in its people.

Changing centuries

History is not only unfolding before our eyes: it is unfolding within us. My hope is that readers of this book will realize that they themselves are part of this tormented destiny, giving birth to a new century. Rather than reducing it to abstractions, may these pages make Europe visible, allow ideas to mature from facts rather than sink into the nothingness of numbers and dogma. May thought once again become an adventure steeped in reality rather than an escape or abstraction like Ulysses's curiosity as he sets sail on the uncertain sea.

At the source of our reflections, a certain sensibility is asserting itself: that of a youth far removed from the idols of the old century - our *ancien régime*, as it were. The page we are turning bears a name often confused: *liberalism*. Here, we need to be clear, and Jean-Claude Michéa's contribution to the question seems decisive.[5] Liberalism is leaving history

---

Orbán. It was here in 2014 that he defended the democratic establishment of an "illiberal state."

[5] "There can be little doubt that if Adam Smith or Benjamin Constant were to return to us ... they would have the greatest difficulty in recognizing the rose of their liberalism in the cross of the present. Hence, no doubt, the incredible intellectual confusion that now reigns unchallenged in the use of this word ... Thus, for many, a distinction should be made between 'good' political and cultural liberalism and 'bad' economic liberalism; and criticism of the latter should itself be nuanced according to whether we are dealing with 'true' liberalism, 'neo-liberalism' or 'ultraliberalism.' The thesis I intend to defend here at least has the merit of simplifying the issue. I maintain that the historical movement that is profoundly transforming modern societies must be fundamentally understood as the logical fulfillment (or truth) of the liberal philosophical project, as it has been progressively defined since the 17th century, and particularly since the Enlightenment. In other words, the soulless world of contemporary capitalism is the only historical form in which this original liberal doctrine could be realized in practice." Jean-Claude Michéa, *L'empire du moindre mal*, Climats, 2006.

for what it has become. Western youth is drinking its dregs; it has seen only the shadows of the virtues it was supposed to embody. It is up to the new generation to disdain those principles that have been made into psalms, and to whose song they are led to the slaughterhouse, if not to the abyss.

This "illiberal" catharsis is tantamount to freeing ourselves from the twentieth century, and Central Europe stands out as the region of Europe best qualified to show us the way. Indeed, its constituent countries were neither the genesis nor the main players in any of the ideologies that tore Europe apart: communism, liberalism, fascism.

Ideologies are intellectual products, endowed with perishable qualities, between which a choice has to be made. It is a recipe: ready-to-civilize. But the very notion of ideology is foreign to us. That a human brain should try to understand the finer points of collective existence seems to us an imposture; the individual cannot subjugate the group. That an enlightened generation should have definitively grasped the truth, disregarding the centuries of which it is the heir, in order to condition all posterity, is the absurdity from which Europe must emerge today. We are not judging the twentieth century: we are turning our backs on it. If it is still with us, it is because it is determined to destroy what is eternal in us. We need to rediscover our solid foundations.

An enemy of ideologies cannot propose a new one. I do not pretend to reveal the truth. My aim is simply to familiarize the reader with a *kairos* that is, on the whole, favorable for Europe and its nations so that they once again fit into the *chronos*, to return our civilization to essential continuities, to reconnect with an order that reconciles a taste for action with a sense of the unchanging, to reconcile us with trends that elevate us and call us to live.

I.

What is Central Europe?

It is not enough to present a statesman through his political career; the facts must also be placed in their historical context, which explains them as much as they prolong it. There is no point in recounting the history of Central Europe here. An abridged account would only remind specialists of the centuries. We prefer a fragment that exposes the essential: the tragic condition of peoples who are both unique and too weak to survive in isolation. The Czechs faced Germanic hegemony. The Hungarians faced Ottoman conquest. The Poles faced Russian domination and threats from other empires. If Central Europe exists, it is because the nations that make it up have all lived through "the same great common existential experience: that of a nation choosing between its existence and its non-existence; in other words, between its authentic national life and assimilation into a larger nation."[6] One period invites us to grasp for each people its failed assertion of political exclusivity – and the abnegation of an authentic national life. That these experiences predate ideological setbacks adds to their value: a national consciousness matured in adversity then faced up to the perils of the contemporary era.

Double membership

Slavs populated Bohemia and Moravia as early as the fifth century, becoming Czechs. The Polans joined their tribe with other populations in the Vistula basin, the cradle of Poland. The Magyars, sweeping in from the Pontic steppe at the end of the ninth century, conquered the Carpathian basin under their leader Árpád and soon founded the Kingdom of Hungary.

---

[6] Milan Kundera, *Un Occident kidnappé*, Gallimard, 1984. In this work, the Czech dissident offered a particularly penetrating insight into Central Europe as a distinct region.

A comparison with the kingdom of France immediately reveals the diversity inherent in Europe at the time. France rediscovered in Christianity the Roman unity it had lost since the "great invasions." In the year 1000, the young Capetian kingdom was a land that had been cultivated for many centuries, where Celtic civilization had been Romanized, and where the syncretism of the Pax Romana had absorbed the Germanic populations that established themselves there in the fifth century. France is a land of the Old World ploughed by history. The Carpathian basin has an entirely different destiny. The Danube separated Roman Pannonia from the vast barbarian territories to the north. The unrest at the end of the Western Roman Empire left the region in chaos, with neither the Germans nor the Slavs making their mark. The Magyars conquered the Carpathian Basin around 895. Scattered populations and slaves brought back from their expeditions were subordinated to them. While the Franks assimilated Gaul, the Magyars assimilated the vanquished; the Hungarian language prevailed, and with it the continuity of the nation. Within three centuries, the same people, speakers of an original language and commanded by the same warrior aristocracy, joined peoples who had been Romanized for a thousand years throughout medieval civilization. This disparity indicates two things. First, the eminently European character of the Hungarians, who entered the European order as successfully as they did[7] with a Roman clergy to frame this tumultuous society, a warrior nobility, and a people who were hardly peasants, in love with their land no less than any other European ploughman. Second, the irresistible power of European civilization, which was able to form a family of such diverse elements. Indeed, it is one of the wonders of history that Western Christendom was so great as to embrace original peoples and peoples gathered together to launch them in concert into the beautiful medieval centuries.

In Bohemia and Poland, as in Hungary, if the aristocracy rallied to the Cross and entered into a Western alliance system, it was to maintain itself, not to deny it. The continuation of these peoples in the Christian order is

---

[7] The tripartite organization of medieval society was theorized by Adalbéron de Laon, Archbishop of Rheims, at the beginning of the eleventh century. It distinguishes between those who pray, those who fight, and those who work.

reminiscent of the German case, with three nuances: the Germanic world had been imbued with Roman references on its southern and western flanks since the High Empire, its size has preserved a great deal of internal diversity and, above all, it has incorporated itself into the Christian West to take the lead. In both cases, however, symbolic, religious sovereignty was sacrificed to secure recognition of effective, political sovereignty in the *Respublica Christiana*.[8]

Catholic Europe brings together peoples who are ethnolinguistically related, but this kinship is no guarantee of understanding: that understanding came from the elements born of common belonging to the Christian West, which give these countries mature traits.

Primitive identity was gradually enriched by the leaven of history. The family bond at the root of social order found its political incarnation in the prestige of a family that became a metaphor for the nation: the dynasty. As institutions became more complex and political, the analogy between family, dynasty, and nation became more symbolic. This phenomenon made a decisive contribution to the formation of European countries and of Europe as a whole, as illustrated by the kinship links between the Houses of France and Bohemia in the fourteenth century. Dynastic continuity sublimated the "tribalism" of peoples, and accompanied a complexification and exaltation of political order. By the end of their medieval maturation, the nations of Central Europe had assimilated Roman civilization without losing their originality. So it was no longer peoples who met, but countries that rubbed shoulders. The Visegrád meeting, which gave its name to today's Visegrád Group, provides an illuminating insight into what Central Europe was like 700 years ago.

The event took place in 1335. Thirty kilometers north of Buda, in his

---

[8] Medieval Christianity can be seen as a renewal of Romanization, marked not by the SPQR sign (*Senatus populusque romanus*: the Senate and the Roman people), but by the Cross. The first Romanization was marked by the political conversion of conquered peoples, formalized by the annual sacrifice to the Emperor, beyond which the plurality of the divine was recognized. The second Romanization involved rallying to a Christianity adapted to the sensibilities of the European peoples. This Romanization no longer stumbled, but was supported by the Germanic world since Charlemagne had united it under his scepter. At the same time, the East came under the authority of Islam, a third force in the face of Orthodox Christianity, inexorably ousted from its Byzantine cradle and transferred to Moscow when Constantinople fell in 1453.

castle overlooking the Danube, Charles-Robert of Hungary received the Bohemian King John I and the Polish King Casimir III. This was a time when the Přemyslids (1306) and the Árpáds (1301), the national dynasties that had integrated Bohemia and Hungary into the European order, had come to an end. John I of Bohemia reached an agreement with the King of Poland to determine their respective zones of influence: the King of Bohemia dropped his ambitions for Poland, and Casimir III abandoned his claims to Lusatia and Silesia. These measures were taken to defend their interests against two ambitious Germanic powers: Austria to the south and the Teutonic Order to the north. The Francophile King of Bohemia, of Luxembourgish and Flemish descent, made policy for his nation, not for himself. Under the mantle of a still united Christendom, the rising national fact took shape.

Bohemia in the Holy Roman Empire

The clearest and earliest example of national assertion can be found in Bohemia. There is a simple reason for this: the Kingdom of Bohemia was an integral part of the Holy Roman Empire,[9] i.e. within the political framework of the German lands. This Western orientation was definitive. After two centuries of continuous assertion, the Golden Bull of Sicily, promulgated by Frederick II of Hohenstaufen in 1212, established Bohemia's privileged position within the Empire. The royal title became hereditary; its holder was granted, among other privileges, the right to appoint the kingdom's bishops and to appear only at diets convened by the Emperor.

Germanic populations exerted considerable influence in the Czech lands. Parallel to the political construction of Bohemia-Moravia, the medieval period was marked by an extraordinary German dynamism: the *Drang nach Osten* or "drive to the east." While the Czechs cultivated the country's most hospitable region, central Bohemia, the border regions remained virtually empty of people. Peasants were gradually moving in. This was not colonization by Germany, but simply an expansion of

---

[9] The Holy Roman Empire (800-1806) was a major institution in European history: not only the political framework of feudal Germany, but also the renewal of the Roman Empire and the Carolingian Empire. In 950, even before Otto I acceded to the imperial dignity, the Czech duke Boleslav I submitted to the powerful King of Germany.

Christianity. This movement continued until the thirteenth century.[10] The agrarian revolution led to the growth of towns, where the patriciate was predominantly German. The mining towns, by developing lucrative export-oriented activities, ensured the emergence of the Czech lands on the European stage. Finally, the nobility was the driving force behind Bohemia's "Europeanization." Chivalric fashions, born in the South of France in the twelfth century, penetrated Central Europe as far as Prague, notably via Thuringia. Medieval scholasticism and classical literature spread a common European culture. It was also among the nobility that the drama of German influence at the heart of the Czech nation was played out. As part of alliance policies, Czech nobles took German princesses as wives, introducing Germanic traditions.

This concomitant maturation of the nation and Western Christianity was a crucial phenomenon throughout the region, culminating in the Czech lands during the reign of Charles I of Bohemia (1346-1378). His reign was marked by peace and a general flourishing of the country, miraculously spared the Black Death. Prague doubled in size under his reign and was adorned with monuments that are still admired today. At this time, largely German-speaking provinces such as Silesia, Lusatia, and Brandenburg came under the Bohemian crown. The strengthening of the monarchy set the country on the path to a political franchise almost equal to that of Poland and Hungary. Bohemia asserted itself as the Empire's center of gravity, while Prague shone as the intellectual capital of the other non-Germanic countries in the region.

The crumbling of the medieval order threatened this prosperous kingdom, which was about to sink into religious divisions, political chaos and, ultimately, foreign domination. From this point of view, Bohemia deserves to be considered as the first European country to confront the problems of the modern period, which was marked by denominational and national issues. A dynastic friendship linked the kingdoms of France and

---

[10] It led to an agrarian and demographic revolution. German settlers introduced the so-called "Magdeburg law," under which the lord guaranteed certain rights and authorized the use of the land in exchange for the payment of cash royalties by the community. The intermediary in these operations, a "locator," took charge of populating virgin territories and collecting the sums demanded. To attract settlers, the landowner sometimes grants tax exemptions.

Bohemia in the fourteenth century: the political modernization under Charles I of Bohemia was inspired by his French upbringing. But the French impetus was shattered by the Black Death and the Hundred Years' War; in Bohemia, competition between Czechs and Germans spurred the assertion of national sentiment. This was fueled by religious issues arising from the Great Western Schism (1378-1415), theological controversies, and clerical disorders. Theological innovations came from England (John Wycliffe's theses), while opposition to Papal prerogatives generally came from Germanic and French sovereigns. But Bohemia stood out as the most mature country, articulating national and religious issues in an unprecedented way.

This long-awaited bomb exploded through the fate of Czech reformer Jan Hus.[11] The Hussite wars (1417-1437) triggered by the reformer's martyrdom inflicted the first tear in the mantle of Catholicism, and exposed the Czechs to the ambitions of their neighbors. This was not just a religious fever (like the Cathar or Waldensian heresies), but an attempt to nationalize religion a century before Martin Luther in Germany and Henry VIII in England.

But it was too early, or Bohemia was too small. Divisions between Catholics and Hussites, and among the latter between different sensibilities (Utraquists, Taborites, etc.) undermined the country. These divisions became even more pronounced in the following century with the Reformation. In two hundred years, marked by periods of attrition and revival, Bohemia went from absolute freedom supported by its arms to complete subordination to the House of Austria and its Habsburg rulers.

The Hussite wars ended with a compromise: the *Compactata*. In 1458, the Czech George of Poděbrady (1420-1471) was elected king by the Diet; the crown of St. Wenceslas thus regained complete freedom and a certain stability. But dynastic alliances inevitably favored the Habsburg neighbor. The combined advantages of imperial dignity, geographical proximity, and Germanic power irresistibly drew Prague into Vienna's fold. The

---

[11] Jan Hus was born in 1369 and died in 1415. The literary importance of his translation of the Scriptures into common language, his immense success as a theologian, rector of the University of Prague and preacher, and his political influence, culminating in his condemnation to the stake at the Council of Constance, elevated him to the pinnacle of national history. Hus is a pivotal figure in Czech, if not European, history.

Austrian rulers' skillful policy was further enhanced by historical circumstances.

Louis II of Hungary died in 1526 as the Ottoman army conquered his country. But he was also King of Bohemia and a close relative of the Archduke of Austria, Ferdinand I: the latter thus inherited both crowns and the decisive role of Christianity's bulwark against Islam. This exceptional situation gave Ferdinand access to north-west Hungary without a blow being struck; it also enabled him to demand numerous extraordinary contributions from Bohemia to contain the Ottoman thrust and gave the Habsburgs hereditary rights over the subordinate crowns. It is easy to see how the freedoms of Central European countries are intertwined, and how they are doomed to succumb if they fail to support each other.

Since 1517, Luther's Reformation had been spreading throughout Europe, and in Bohemia religious conflicts had been rekindled. The Habsburgs became champions of the Catholic Church. Tolerance of the Hussites and Protestants, whose divisions strengthened Vienna's power, fluctuated. In 1618, a restriction of Protestant rights led to the second "Defenestration of Prague," the event that triggered the dreadful Thirty Years' War.[12] Emperor Ferdinand II decided to subdue the Czechs: the Battle of White Mountain (1620) marked the beginning of the nation's "Dark Ages." Bohemia became the personal property of the House of Habsburg and would never again resist armed invasion.

Slovakia's "infra-state" history deserves our attention below.

Hungary and the Ottoman Empire n

In contrast to the ambivalence of German-Czech relations, a clear antagonism characterized the Turkish-Hungarian face-off. Ottoman power had been a source of concern for Europe since the eleventh century, when Turkish abuses in the Holy Land prompted the first Crusade. The battlefield shifted from Asia to Europe in 1346, when the Ottomans seized Gallipoli, a town on the European side of the Hellespont. Moving deeper into Europe, the Ottomans isolated Byzantium from the Balkans, where

---

[12] From 1618 to 1648. A major event in Central European history, this international conflict led to the fragmentation of the Germanic world (Treaties of Westphalia, 1648) and French continental hegemony.

their raids multiplied – a Hungarian-Turkish skirmish was already reported in 1366 near the Iron Gates.[13] Crusades and campaigns followed one another on European soil for centuries, powerless to stem the irresistible ascendancy of the Ottoman Empire. The Ottoman Empire reached its peak between the sieges of Vienna in 1529 and 1683. Europe, unable to present a united front, succumbed to the Turks until such unity was reached. Following in the footsteps of the divided Balkan peoples, Hungary paid for its unequal duel with the East in the sixteenth and seventeenth centuries, from which it has never fully recovered.

The face-off between the Ottomans and the Hungarians before the defeat at Mohács in 1526 illustrated three trends leading the country to disaster: disdain for the Orthodox Balkans, the vagaries of succession, and disordered ambition.

*

The Capetian dynasty of Anjou-Sicily succeeded the Arpadian dynasty, which died out in 1301. Charles-Robert I (1288-1342) not only enriched his kingdom with Italian influence, but also forged a privileged alliance with Venice and used the Dalmatian coast as the basis for an ambitious maritime policy. Hungary could then join forces with its Balkan neighbors, as outlined by the marriage of heir Louis I (1326-1382) to Elisabeth of Bosnia in 1353. But the gulf between the Catholic and Orthodox worlds could not easily be bridged, and Hungary's prestige heralded the expansion of Central Europe to the south, rather than a nascent unity between the Balkans and the West. The heart of the fourteenth century was, moreover, a period of prosperity for the Serbs, and misfortune would have it that incidents would later occupy the Hungarians to the north and the Serbs to the south at the same time. The Polish throne was promised to Louis I in the absence of a male heir. This prospect, which became a reality in 1370, led Hungary into a Polish policy, taking part in crusades against the Lithuanians at a time of early Turkish success. When the Byzantine emperor John V Palaeologus offered his conversion to Catholicism in a bid for the Hungarian king's help, the latter bowed to the Pope's defiance and devoted himself to the Kingdom of Poland until his death in 1382.

---

[13] cf. Louis Léger, *Histoire de l'Autriche-Hongrie*, 1879.

In two battles, Maritsa in 1371 and Kosovo Pole in 1389, the Balkan powers were defeated: Serbia, reduced to a vassal of the Ottoman Empire, retained a degree of autonomy; Wallachia acknowledged its tributary status to the Turks; Bulgaria was invaded. Only Byzantium remained.

*

Sigismund of Luxembourg (1368-1437) was a younger son of the great King Charles I of Bohemia, whom we have already met. Two years after his election to the Hungarian throne, the defeat at Kosovo Polje convinced him of the imminent Ottoman threat, and he decided to organize a European crusade. The army left Buda in July 1396. The crusaders trampled on besieged Nicopolis on the Bulgarian side of the Danube. Discipline slackened, and the unexpected arrival of a Turkish army at the end of September resulted in a resounding defeat. By this time, the Balkans were a zone of divided influence. Byzantium was still holding out thanks to its fleet and ramparts, while Catholic Europe was divided by the Great Western Schism and the Hundred Years' War. The Hungarians had to face up to the situation on their own, and organized the famous hussar units, specially designed to fight the Ottomans. To the same end, Sigismund I founded the Order of the Dragon in 1408. But he soon obtained the imperial dignity, then became King of Bohemia upon the death of his brother. This enormous accumulation of responsibilities kept the sovereign busy with countless tasks, and relegated Hungary to the fringe, a mere annex to the Germanic central corps. As emperor, he tried to heal the schism between Rome and Avignon, then devoted himself unsuccessfully to putting an end to the Hussite wars, all at a time when the Ottoman threat was growing. The king's imperial title was of no help to the Hungarians. To the contrary, as emperor, he declared war on Venice and was finally forced to cede Dalmatia, which was Hungarian, to Venice.

*

Before the sad epilogue of independent Hungary, two fine figures in European annals embellish Hungarian history in its heyday: John Hunyadi (1407-1456) and Mathias I the Just (1443-1490). The prowess of Jean Hunyadi, a Transylvanian warlord and later regent of Hungary, raised hopes for the reconquest of the Balkans. He repulsed a Turkish army in

Transylvania, near Sibiu, then crushed it at the Iron Gates in 1442. In July 1443, the Hungarians raced south, capturing Niš and Sofia, then crushing the Turkish army in the Maritsa basin. The road to Constantinople - still Christian for a few years - was open. But far from their bases and with winter approaching, the Hungarians accepted the peace offered by Sultan Murad. The Szeged Diet set the following conditions: the truce would last ten years, Wallachia would come under Hungarian suzerainty, Serbia and Herzegovina would be returned to Turkish suzerainty, and Turkish prisoners would be ransomed. Cardinal Julian Cesarini nevertheless convinced the Hungarian Diet to override the sworn peace to drive the Turks out of the Balkans once and for all.

The battle of Varna, on November 10, 1444, turned to the Sultan's advantage. A new campaign four years later failed on the Kosovo plain, with the Christians still fighting outnumbered. The capture of Byzantium in 1453 galvanized the Ottomans, who laid siege to Belgrade, the key to Western Christendom, in 1456. Jean Hunyadi victoriously defended the city and pursued the enemy as far as Sofia, thanks to volunteers rallied by the monk John of Capistrano. These successes were to have no lasting effect, and Jean Hunyadi died shortly afterwards. Pope Pius II declared: "Our hopes died with him."

The fight against the Turks resumed under the reign of Mátyás Hunyadi (1458-1490), John's youngest son. After several successes, Mathias granted a truce to Sultan Bajazet and turned against Austria.

Before succumbing to foreign interference, Hungary had itself interfered in the politics of neighboring states. Far from supporting Bohemia's independence under George of Poděbrady, Mathias took advantage of its weakness. Under the pretext of fighting the Hussites, he seized territories from the Crown. In so doing, he not only lost an ally willing to join the fight against the Ottomans, but also alienated the Emperor, since attacking Bohemia was tantamount to meddling in imperial affairs. Mathias fought on three fronts: within Bohemia and against Austria and the Ottomans. The King of Hungary defeated the Habsburgs, taking Vienna after a siege in 1485. In vain he left the following epitaph at his death: "Austria defeated attests to my strength. I was the terror of the world; the Emperor of Germany and the Emperor of the Turks trembled before me; only death could defeat me."

The vagaries of succession and the illusion of invincibility led Hungary to disaster. Benign during the reign of Louis I, worrying under Sigismund, the election of foreign kings proved dramatic during the last 35 years of independent Hungary. Particularly in an elective monarchy, the king is not the dispenser but the guarantor of the nation's political rights, which are symbolized by the Crown. Succession, or election, authorizes the coronation ceremony, conferring sovereignty on the king. The hereditary nature of monarchies in Europe has enabled the construction of perennial and powerful states, whose government requires exceptional qualities. The absence of a male heir led to the succession of a monarch who was certainly related to the family, but unfamiliar with the complexities of the country where he was to personify order and whose weakness left him open to the aristocratic factions he was supposed to dominate; religious quarrels multiplied this political instability. From 1490 to 1516, the crown of Hungary fell to Vladislas IV of Bohemia, who was already struggling to govern his first country. His son, Louis II, succeeded him on a regular basis: but he was only ten years old when he came to the throne, and party rule undermined Hungary's position on the Ottoman volcano. The country's fate was sealed on the battlefield of Mohács, in 1526.

Medieval Hungary did not anticipate the formation of the great groups that Central Europe would have to confront. It failed to find a definitive solution to the Turkish threat, which could only be resolved by removing it from Europe, while Austria and the Hussites simply needed to be contained. As a result, Hungary was isolated. The Turks were extending a foreign world into Europe, in which the peoples of Europe had no political horizon, where their civilization found no resources, and where the only future lay in leaving.

Poland between Moscow and Berlin

In some respects, Poland is Hungary's twin sister. Both nations joined Christianity around the year 1000 and assimilated into the Latinate order. Both enjoyed complete political freedom outside the imperial bosom, the nerve of which lay in the landed aristocracy.

The destinies of the two countries diverged in three stages from the late fourteenth century onwards. While the collapse of the Serbs at the battle of Kosovo Pole (1389) exposed Hungary to the Turks, Poland joined forces with the Grand Duchy of Lithuania (1386) to oppose the encroachments of the Teutonic Knights. At this time, Lithuania extended into old territories of Kievan Russia, giving the Polish-Lithuanian dyarchy assets of a great power. This was followed by the important victory over the Teutonic Order at Tannenberg (1410).

At a time when the valiant efforts of John Hunyadi could not prevent the fall of Byzantium, Poland launched a thirteen-year war against the Teutonic Order, culminating in the Second Peace of Thorn in 1466. The order was forced to cede Danzig, Pomerania, and several commanderies to the Polish king, while recognizing itself as his vassal for its remaining territories. The Teutonic Order was reluctant to pay homage to its suzerain, but a third circumstance confirmed Polish hegemony in Northern Europe.

Sensitive to Luther's theses, the Grand Master of the Teutonic Order, Albert of Brandenburg, embraced the Reformation. He secularized the order and thus founded Europe's first Protestant state. Banished from the Empire by Charles V, he was forced to turn to his Polish suzerain, Sigismund I, and secured his support in exchange for the homage he paid him in April 1525. Poland thus fanned the flames of division in its Germanic neighborhood; it also broke Catholic unity from within, a year before the Ottoman invasion of Hungary undermined it from without: in 150 years, the twin kingdoms of Central Europe had lost almost all points of comparison.

Poland would later discover its tragic destiny: the sixteenth century was golden on the banks of the Vistula. Favorable economic conditions allowed the fruits of the Renaissance to flourish. The shores of the Baltic were thriving in their old commercial habits. The German world was exhausted in confessional quarrels, and Muscovy was slowly rallying the Russian world under its control. Poland's heyday was marked by the union of Lublin in 1569, when it merged with Lithuania to form the Republic of Two Nations. This act of union conferred on the Lithuanian nobility the prerogatives accorded to the Polish nobility; both now sat together in the Sejm in Warsaw, replacing the diets of Kraków and Vilnius. Royal Prussia and Danzig came fully under the authority of the new state.[14]

These remarkable assets did not, however, result in a French-style centralization and government by *raison d'état*. Far from restricting the role of the nobility, as the Valois and Bourbons did in France, the Polish monarchy yielded to the pressure of noble demands. From the outset, the monarchy and nobility had been reciprocating services: military devotion in exchange for political prerogatives. This unbreakable alliance kept the German urban patriciate at bay at home and the Teutonic military threat at bay abroad. The nobility – known as the *szlachta* – formed the legally empowered country; their military and land power preserved their taste for freedom and country ways. In the heyday of prosperity, however, the nobility prepared for the political paralysis of the country by fiercely defending its privileges.

Poland was no stranger to war with the Turks. The south of the vast republic was regularly raided by the Crimean Tatars, vassals of the Sublime Porte. The late triumph of the Counterreformation led Poland to become more involved with the Ottomans. The latter had attempted to invade the Republic of Two Nations in 1621 and again in 1633, but without success beyond the Carpathian Mountains. Above all, the Turks' second siege of Vienna, in 1683, was lifted thanks to the help of John III Sobieski's Polish army. The Battle of Kahlenberg, on September 12, 1683, marked the first step in the inexorable retreat of the Turks, who were soon expelled from the Kingdom of Hungary by the brilliant Eugene of Savoy.

At the same time, modern Russia entered the European scene with a bang. Peter the Great, who came to the throne in 1682, built a capital on the Baltic Sea, St. Petersburg, which soon eclipsed Sweden's northern hegemony. From the outset, Poland was Moscow's competitor because of its sovereignty over traditionally Orthodox lands. Poland's identification with Catholicism led to the creation of the Uniate Church in 1596, which brought many peasants from Belarus and Ukraine into the Roman fold while Orthodox religious rites remained respected. The extension of Latinate culture eastwards via Poland challenged a previous confessional boundary. Combined with the harsh living conditions, Roman proselytism led to frequent revolts increasingly led by the Cossack state, which owed

---

[14] Daniel Bauvois, *Histoire de la Pologne*, Le Seuil, 2010.

no firm allegiance to any surrounding power. The conflict became international, as the Crimean Tatars supported the insurrection, and Moscow took advantage of the turmoil to seize control of the left bank of the Dnieper in 1648. In the year when the Treaties of Westphalia brought peace to Germany, Poland retreated from Moscow for the first time, with Ukraine's submission to Moscow at least theoretically following in the Union of Pereiaslav (1654). Slavic and Catholic at the same time, Poland weakened at a time when Prussia began to expand its influence in Germany and Moscow both emerged as the unifier of Russia and extended its rule over subject peoples all the way to the Pacific. The former prefigured German unity, the latter Russian Orthodox unity: two huge and lasting shadows cast over Poland until recent times.

The country's long decline led to the first partition of Poland in 1772. The border regions to the east and northwest, populated mainly by Orthodox on one side and Germans on the other, passed into the hands of Russia and Prussia, respectively. As "compensation," Austria took over Galicia, the region bordering the Kingdom of Hungary, where the peasantry was largely Ukrainian. The vice tightened on the remaining core. France, in the midst of its revolution, was unable to prevent the complete dismemberment of Poland in 1792 and 1794, which further strengthened the partitioning powers and wiped an independent Poland off the map until 1918.

Much of Poland remained under Russian domination and was subjected to increasingly harsh rule, from a simple protectorate to an attempt to absorb it into the bosom of a power that was certainly Slavic, but profoundly foreign. Russian elites cherished the dream of bringing their "lost" brothers back to the homeland of all Slavs. In response to the Polish uprisings of 1830, 1848, and 1863, St. Petersburg tightened its grip on national freedoms. As in Hungary's case with the Ottoman Empire, Poles felt alienated from their homeland in the Russian Empire. The writer Kasimierz Brandys lamented in another era of subjection, that of the Cold War: "Russian destiny is not part of our consciousness; it is foreign to us; we are not responsible for it. It weighs on us, but it is not our heritage ... I would prefer not to know their world, not to know that it exists."[15]

---

[15] Kasimierz Brandys, *Miesiące*, 1982-1984. Quoted in Milan Kundera, op. cit.

The west of the former Republic of the Two Nations retained more of its franchise under Prussian rule. It was here that the uprising of 1848 was organized, before spreading throughout the country. But German unity, achieved in 1870, led to a tightening of the German yoke and an attempt to Germanize the Polish population.

Only in Austria did the situation evolve towards greater autonomy after a long reactionary period. It was not the uprisings of 1848-1849, but the Prussian victory over Austria at Sadowa (1866) that triggered the change. First, German unity was achieved not only without Austria, but on its back; second, the loss of prestige for Vienna forced Emperor Franz Joseph to redistribute the cards within the empire to the benefit of non-German populations. The result was the Austro-Hungarian Compromise of 1867 and the deepening of the empire's multi-national character, from which the Poles, among others, benefited.

*

To summarize, Bohemia, undermined by internal divisions, was subjugated by Austria. Hungary, vanquished as an independent power and partially restored under the Habsburgs, became part of a supranational Danubian entity. Poland discovered its limits in the face of the great Russian and German entities on either side. This absence of projection is indeed a turn of civilization, a historical education whose opposite example can be found in Western Europe: while Hungary was fading at Mohács, Spain conquered Mexico and Peru. While France was theorizing about the nature of mankind in the eighteenth century, Poland squashed by Russia, Prussia, and Austria. Both before and after the fall of the Austrian eagle, Central Europe was two-headed, that is, nourished by both an original consciousness and a civilizational heritage. Thus united under the sign of the *limit*, Central Europe's tutelary goddess was Athena.[16] Strongly aware of a troubled past and a future in potential peril, this Europe is questioning the EU at the turn of the 2020s.

---

[16] Also known as "The Pensive Athena," this fifth-century B.C. statue depicts the goddess gazing at a milestone, expressing the limit. Excess, on the other hand, was in ancient Greek eyes the worst vice.

II.

First steps in the rubble

At the opposite end of the Central European spectrum, Viktor Orbán has been favored by fate. His youthful commitment to opposing Soviet domination coincided with the collapse of the Yalta settlement, and Russia moved away from the Carpathian basin for good. Twenty years later, the structural crisis of the liberal West gave him room for maneuver, which he skillfully exploited to build an illiberal state. The favorable circumstances allowed Viktor Orbán's political career a meteoric rise.

Although insufficient to explain such success, we can recognize the champion of illiberalism's solid political qualities: a flair for action and the use of power and an awareness of both his abilities and his limitations. He has an intimate, popular disposition to understand what is being done and what is not and a common decency served by an aptitude for action and power visible in a country of ten million inhabitants. His detractors define him as an autocrat. No doubt a propensity to use power characterizes him, but the revolution that he carries within him is to aspire to power in order to submit it to an authority that surpasses him. Viktor Orbán wishes to return Hungary and Europe, lost in the maze of exhausted ideologies, to a traditional order, to rediscover the peace of the centuries before the turmoil of the years, the soul of the people above the whims of corrupted generations, the continuity of a civilization despite the ideological gaps that have scarred it. His titanic personality is therefore hardly tainted by suspicion.

Viktor Orbán is of average height. For a long time, playing soccer on a regular basis kept him athletic. His image has become much stronger since his return to power in 2010. His hair has lost its brown color, but his face retains the same character. Viewed from three quarters, the nasal bridge extends into the two graying eyebrows, which slope like oblique eagles toward the temples, giving the face its singular unity. You can guess how much the ideas under the brow owe to the flair that fires them up. A man of instinct and character above all, he asserts: "In politics, you have to act. You can't weigh, evaluate, plan, or worry about what's going to happen. If you feel something needs to be done, do it! Intellectuals are too thoughtful. They see too many obstacles. In politics, two characteristics are detrimental: if you're too smart and if you're not smart enough."[17] Beneath the eyebrows, the head of government's sparkling, scrutinizing eyes retain glints of *bonhommie*. The inflections of his gaze betray a long experience of life and an extraordinary vitality. His voice exudes authority, and the rumbly, rattling sound of Hungarian strikes the foreign listener, surprised to find such aplomb in such an unusual language. This is because Hungary, like its Prime Minister, invites us to travel and demands that we strip ourselves of cumbersome habits and ready-made ideas.

An anti-communist dissident

Viktor Orbán was born on May 31, 1963, in Székesfehérvár, a town close to his family's village, Felcsút. Fate's first gift to Orbán was to offer him no comforts, but a childhood full of challenges and rural simplicity. He did not have running water until he entered high school. The Orbáns lived in a house at the end of the village, which attests to their working-class status, a situation that hardened young Viktor. He has a fighting temperament. He pulls no punches and goes against the tide. Charles Péguy once wrote that everything in us is decided before we reach the age of twelve. From childhood, Orbán developed a real passion for soccer. His passion for the game was spontaneous. His interaction with great numbers of people was never lacking, and he cultivated throughout his life this inclination for the people he came from, and his ability to be understood by them. His second lucky star was the presence in the Orbán household of Mihail Sipos, his maternal grandfather. Between grandfather and grandson, a decisive understanding was born. This relationship with his grandfather enabled Orbán to grasp all that the Hungarian province of

---

[17] Igor Janke, *Napastnik. Opowieść o Viktorze Orbánie*, 2012. Unless otherwise stated, quotes from Viktor Orbán are taken from the essay, in its English version: *Forward! The Story of Hungarian Prime Minister Viktor Orbán*, Aeramentum, 2015.

the 1960s concealed about eternal Hungary. Beneath the socialist veneer[18] breathes an unspoiled rural culture, not unlike the Burgundy of *The War of the Buttons*. It's still the old, living Christendom.

*

Viktor Orbán's remarkable liveliness prompted his parents to set him on an ambitious course. At the end of elementary school, he took the entrance exam for the English-speaking section of the renowned Gymnasium Teleki Blanka in Székesfehérvár. His success was a welcome surprise for a child of modest origins. The Gymnasium occupies an imposing building that radiates the prosperity and aristocratic elegance of Central Europe, in the image of Countess Teleki Blanka, who gave her name to the school built in the late nineteenth century. Székesfehérvár is a royal town – the name literally means "the seat of the white fortress." Its basilica was built in the sixteenth century. It witnessed the coronation of 43 Hungarian kings and houses the remains of 15 of them. It owes its Baroque style to the reconstruction undertaken at the end of the Ottoman occupation. Székesfehérvár harbors the past grandeur of the Hungarian kingdom and taught Viktor Orbán the mediocrity of the socialist regime. As he says: "High school was the very first step in my life towards anti-communism."[19] The regime's censorship was very light, however. High school students had access to magazines which, while never attacking socialism head-on, covered a wide range of ideas. Viktor and a few of his classmates organized meetings devoted to press reviews and debates. Political awareness was quietly awakened in the protective, polite environment of the provincial high school. But this calm preceded the turmoil of military service that awaited all men in the Hungarian People's Republic as they entered adulthood.

In the summer of 1981, Orbán began eleven-and-a-half months of military service. The year he spent in garrison service was the decisive stage in his transition to anti-communism. At the time, the Hungarian army was one of the most poorly organized forces in the Soviet-led Warsaw

---

[18] In this case, his father, Győző Orbán, was a member of the Communist Party. This membership contributed to the family's social rise.
[19] Igor Janke, ibidem, p. 42

Pact. Orbán's regiment was stationed in Zalaegerszeg, a pretty Transdanubian town between Lake Balaton and the Austrian border.

Military service was a catch-up session for comrades reluctant to embrace communism. The harsh, clumsy propaganda of the staff soon exasperated conscripts like Orbán, whose skepticism of the system quickly turned to detestation: "It was in Zalaegerszeg that it became clear to me that the state was badly organized, and that change was necessary."[20] It also cemented strong friendships. A blond, elegant young man agreed on everything with the foot soldier Viktor Orbán: the artilleryman Gabor Fodor, who accompanied him through his student life to the founding of Fidesz and into the early days of post-socialist Hungary. The pressure on the strong-headed young men was all the greater, for they were encouraged to join the party. Once in, they were entitled to privileges and positions of responsibility. These maneuvers seduced some and aroused a deep aversion in others.

The most intense moment of his year in the army came in December 1981, when Poland was in turmoil. The huge Solidarność movement nearly toppled the communist regime in Warsaw. The armies of the Eastern Bloc stood ready to intervene. The Zalaegerszeg garrison received its mobilization order on December 11. Departure was imminent: the Polish crowd had to be subdued in order to fall into line. Orbán, who greatly admired the Polish dissidents, mourned his likely duty, but the proclamation of martial law in Poland two days later ruled out the possibility of foreign intervention. Solidarność rekindled the hopes of East European youth. Orbán used it as a reference point for his own political action. On June 12, 1987, he found himself in Gdansk, in the shipyards where Pope John Paul II was giving a mass and openly supporting Lech Wałęsa's movement. Viktor Orbán dedicated his university thesis to Solidarność.

In 1982, Orbán moved to the capital and enrolled in law school at Eötvös Loránd University. He plunged into the whirlwind of student life, in tandem with his friend and roommate Gabor Fodor. They were intelligent, sociable and enterprising; student life offered them all the best aspects of the 1980s in this "most livable shack in the socialist camp," as

---

[20] ibidem, p. 47

Kádár-era Hungary was described. The two friends studied in a privileged setting, a sort of academic principality where professors and students, united by bonds of closeness and esteem, freely organized student life. Their military service at the Abbey of Thélème did little to appease the dissidents' anti-communism. Leonid Brezhnev died on November 10, 1982: a handful of students refused to rise for the minute's silence. Among them were Viktor Orbán and Lajos Simicska. Simicska would play a decisive role for Orbán over the next few years, building up a pro-Fidesz business community in Hungary.

Orbán became president of the student council and excelled at organizing university life, albeit in an authoritarian manner. A memorable clash pitted him against László Kéri, his teacher and future political opponent, who found him intractable. In the spring of 1985, Orbán and his friends managed to fool the university administration. They asked permission to hold the Fourth National Student Meeting at the university. The director imagined that the previous meetings had been legal and made no objection, but this event had no precedent and provided an official forum for dissident youth. There was talk of regime change: every drop erodes the rock.

In 1987, on the advice of their teacher Mr. Felczak, Viktor Orbán and his friends decided to found a political party. On March 30, 1988, at a confused public meeting, the young rebels discussed the initiative. Some of the communists present were outraged at this act, which was carried out under the complaisant eye of intelligence agents, but the majority of those present voted in favor of the formation of an independent political party. This was the birth certificate of the Alliance of Young Democrats, or *Fiatal Demokraták Szövetsége* (Fidesz). The party grew rapidly, from 32 to 1,000 members in one month. It was aimed at young people aged 14 to 35, excluding members of the KISZ (*Magyar Kommunista Ifjúsági Szövetség,* the Hungarian Federation of Young Communists). Fidesz intended to act openly: the age of secrecy was over. Its main goals were to realize a market economy, private property, a multi-party political system, democracy, equality of all citizens, sovereign national policy, protection of Hungarian minorities abroad, and European unity.

An international press conference was held in Budapest on April 6.

The team of six Fidesz spokesmen insisted on the legality of their action. Their sense of justice and the rule of law played an important role in Orbán's political actions. Summoned to appear before the public prosecutor, he was reluctant to comply on the grounds that there was no legal justification for the summons. He later agreed to attend, accompanied by a number of Fidesz leaders, and treated the magistrate casually, quibbling with the judicial authority over legal texts and refusing to identify himself. Orbán did not just extend room for maneuver of the protest, he opened the breach.

The decade of agony for Europe's socialist regimes differed entirely from Western declinism, which had become a veritable science. Writing about "collapse" filled entire shelves in bookshops, acting as a therapy to keep everyone on their toes and nothing changing. When Orbán recalled that he felt the end was near, he said "he would see it in his lifetime." The end of the Eastern bloc remained unthinkable for the vast majority of the population, however,

Orbán's historic good fortune lay in having delivered the most important speech of his life at the age of 26. On June 16, 1989, the reburial ceremony of Imre Nagy and five other dissident ministers executed by Soviet repression in 1956 took place on Heroes' Square in Budapest. Viktor Orbán was chosen to give a speech on behalf of Hungarian youth. With the Eastern bloc still intact, the young Fidesz spokesman called for the withdrawal of Soviet troops from Hungary. Broadcast live on radio and television, the speech aroused a wave of enthusiasm throughout the country and propelled the Felcsút boy into a political career. Orbán didn't just happen to be in the right place at the right time. What foreshadowed his political destiny in this event was the fact that he dared to do something when everyone else was still relying on a wait-and-see attitude or going underground. He broke into the future by freeing himself from a guardianship: that of fear. A few days later, on June 27, the Iron Curtain cracked with the opening of the Austro-Hungarian border. Before the year was out, the Berlin Wall would fall: communism was finally collapsing, and the voice of Hungarian youth had contributed to it. Fidesz acknowledged its debt to Solidarność and the Baltic states, all necessary vectors for the fall of communism in Europe. At the time of the fall of the

Berlin Wall in November 1989, Orbán was already studying political science at Oxford. Like 3,200 Hungarians between 1984 and 1990, he was awarded an Open Society scholarship by a certain George Soros.

Considered the main organization for dissident youth, Fidesz was invited to take part in post-regime negotiations. Orbán then led the Fidesz list in the first free elections, held on March 25 and April 8, 1990, entering Parliament alongside 20 fellow party members.[21] Viktor Orbán has held public office ever since.

Hungary torn apart, or necessary accommodation to the international order

The political context that the Fidesz generation apprehended in 1990 seemed like a vast field of ruins – the twentieth century – after which everything had to be rebuilt. The contrast was the basis of their optimism: the future belonged to them, and yet "if youth is to enjoy the ancient heritage of its fathers, it must conquer it in order to possess it." Goethe's formula indicates the crushing task facing the Fidesz generation. In which Hungary did Viktor Orbán begin his political career? Certainly, in a Western country – it has been one since the year 1000. But for the second time, the disappearance of an Eastern empire had left it in a sorry state, at the mercy of his German neighbor, though this time indirectly, through the organs of European unity. With Germany the continental appendage of the Transatlantic alliance bloc, the destinies of Central Europe seemed inexorably drawn into the wake of the West.

The Cold War victors soon extended their influence eastwards, toward the Orthodox world. Although golden, market democracy took on the appearance of inevitability, as lightning strikes down on those who recoil from it. All the deleterious trends of the century came together in the disastrous wars in Yugoslavia. Nationalism was once again being used as a battering ram for political fragmentation; the rights of peoples masked NATO intervention, which supported separatist Islamic forces on European soil. Liberal aspirations were only leading to a cut-throat

---

[21] Then, in the local elections of autumn 1990, Fidesz emerged as the country's 3ᵉ force with 16% of the vote.

economy that is already bloodless. "Europe died in Pristina,"[22] wrote one witness to the Kosovo War of 1998-1999.

The system in force in the West guarantees private ownership of the means of production and a multi-party system. But beyond that, the same ideological underpinnings prevail as in the East. Where communism is confined to a sequence in Russian history, liberalism in the United States and United Kingdom is a "home-grown" ideology. It is perhaps the only thing that is, given that the Anglo-Saxon countries long benefited from a perpetual becoming guaranteed by divine benevolence and commercial success. This increased America's subversive power tenfold, especially as the countries of Western Europe had no choice but to recognize its pre-eminence.

What matters to Hungarians is to win, even if that means switching from one international system to another. But only the fickle elites pull their weight, obediently relaying Western interests as they once served Moscow; in Hungarian, "regime change" means "gangster change."

Subordination does not mean surrender. Hungarians remember that their nation's survival in Austrian space was once a century-long struggle. If there is a fundamental difference with the reckless Serbia, which was crushed in the dismantling of Yugoslavia, it lies in Hungary's political skill – quite unique in Europe – for negotiating as well as fighting.

*

From the Turkish conquest in 1526 to the expulsion of the Ottomans from Hungary, ratified by the Treaty of Karlowitz in 1699, Hungary experienced various forms of subjection. Transylvania, a vassal state of the Ottoman Empire, retained a large degree of autonomy and, in the eyes of Hungarian historiography, ensured the continuity of an independent national history; the Hungarian plain, up to and including Buda, was under Muslim rule; but in the northwest of the country, which fell under Austrian rule, the relationship that would structure Hungarian history until the First World War began. This part of the country represented the kingdom, since the Archduke of Austria held the crown. The Hungarian orders fought tirelessly to maintain the country's political freedoms or acquire new

---

[22] Reference to the testimony of Jacques Hogard in the eponymous essay *L'Europe est morte à Pristina*, Hugo-Doc, 2014.

prerogatives as the balance of power changed. The seventeenth century, from the Treaty of Vienna (1606) to the Szatmar Compromise (1711), was studded with the ruptures and compromises that founded Central Europe as a negotiated political space.[23] The resulting political education bears witness to the statesmanship, pragmatism and tenacity of the Hungarian elites. Austrian absolutism could not take root in the land of Saint Stephen. The leaders of the rebellions often benefited from the favors of the Habsburg system after a compromise.

This history of conflict, initially between Hungarians who favored accommodation (the *Labancs*) or rupture (the *Kurucs*), bore the seeds of a new equilibrium. According to historian Géza Pálffy: "Through this little-studied series of compromises throughout the seventeenth century, the elite of the Kingdom of Hungary proved that it was possible both to find conciliation with the Habsburg ruler and preserve the fundamental interests of the Hungarian state and orders."[24]

This conciliatory perception of Austro-Hungarian history was illustrated by the construction of Heroes' Square, built during the era of the Dual Monarchy, which featured Austrian sovereigns (Ferdinand I, Charles III, Maria Theresa, Leopold II, and Franz Joseph). In the 1950s, the authorities of socialist Hungary replaced these statues with those of Etienne Bocskai, Gabriel Bethlen, Imre Thököly, François II Rákóczi and Lajos Kossuth: another time, another historiography.

A remarkable singularity is the Hungarians' assertion of good faith in the Central European ensemble that respects them. During the War of the Austrian Succession[25] (1740-1748), Empress Maria Theresa was besieged

---

[23] This gestation was by no means a long, quiet river: Étienne Bocskai's revolt in 1604-1606; the conflicts of 1619-1621; Gabriel Bethlen's campaigns against Ferdinand III in 1623-1624 and 1626; George I Rákóczi's campaigns against Ferdinand III in 1644 and 1645, and the great campaigns of 1660-1664 and 1683-1699. These conflicts, in which Transylvania often revived the Hungarian nobility's desire for independence, gave rise to five new systems of compromise (1608, 1622, 1647, 1681, 1711).

[24] Géza Pálffy, *Les luttes pour l'indépendance et l'unité du royaume: un débat historiographique*, Histoire, économie & société, Armand Colin, 2015.

[25] Charles VI of Habsburg prepared his succession by promulgating the Pragmatic Sanction in 1713. This asserted the indivisibility of the countries of the monarchy and extended the principle of primogeniture in the male line to the female line and to collaterals. In 1740, Maria Theresa ascended the throne. Not recognizing the Pragmatic Sanction, Frederick II of Prussia invaded Silesia without a declaration of war and annexed the province.

from all sides. The Hungarians had the opportunity to stab the beleaguered empress in the back. Instead, they came to her unexpected rescue. At the Diet of Pressburg in 1742, the Hungarians agreed to make a decisive contribution to the war effort in response to Maria Theresa's feminine pleading: 40,000 men, including 15,000 cavalry. In fact, arduous negotiations preceded the agreement, by which the Hungarian Diet obtained satisfaction on a wide range of claims. The result was a united Danubian space, in which Hungary came to terms with Vienna's tutelage, the better to curb it. The rational explanation for this devotion in no way detracts from its poetic power: 22-year-old Marie-Thérèse, recovering from her third pregnancy, came to plead her cause with an infant in her arms. Her vulnerability and grace moved the assembly: with weapon in hand, the Hungarian nobility swore to shed their blood in the phrase that has gone down in history: "*Moriamur pro rege nostro Maria-Theresia!*" ("We will die for our King [sic] Maria Theresa!") This demonstration of Hungarian loyalty aroused admiration throughout Europe and led to a reversal of fortune in this ill-fated war: Prague was recaptured from the French and Saxons, who had taken it after a seven-month siege. At the end of the war, the Habsburg possessions were amputated from rich Silesia, a significant loss that reinforced the importance of the Czech lands and Hungary in Austrian politics, to the detriment of the Germanic element.

*

These historical antecedents help to explain why Viktor Orbán rides the tiger, why oppressive European involvement has never been an option for him, and why he never abandons the perilous alternation of offensives and concessions that has been the ordinary course of Hungarian foreign policy for centuries. Ingenuity entered the service of the simple ambition to live as a Hungarian, which is not a minimalist ambition. At times, Hungarian freedoms seized on favorable circumstances, while at other times the art of consensus fended off imminent peril with a single watchword: not to disappear. Viktor Orbán's entire political career stems from this paradox: extreme political endurance in an increasingly secular and depoliticized Western world.

III.

Asserting a civic Hungary

Neither right nor left

The Budapest Parliament stands on the east bank of the Danube and abuts Lajos Kossuth Square, like a link between the unchanging river and the immortalized leader of the 1848 Revolution. The building was erected between 1885 and 1904, as a majestic statement to Vienna and the world: Hungary intended to assume its destiny. It is an astonishing palace, dedicated to national representation in the illiberal kingdom of St. Stephen.

The Hungarian Parliament illustrates a complex reality and offers useful lessons for sorting out the confused and contradictory notions of reaction and national emancipation, tradition and popular sovereignty. These were all necessary elements in the political maturation of modern Central Europe throughout the nineteenth century. As for the twentieth century, it was to be more a test of drowning in a deluge of ideologies.

*

Let us go back to Hungary's first post-communist elections. The parliamentary majority went to Hungarian Democratic Forum (MDF) led by József Antall. Founded in 1987, this party aimed to push for internal reforms. It was the party of the old right, heavily persecuted since 1944, which in 1990 returned to a country that had been completely turned upside down, and with which it shared only one wish: to put an end to socialism. The wind of history sweeping away the Communists propelled Antall to the post of Prime Minister. Fidesz decided to sit in opposition. There were two reasons for this: a real discrepancy between the conservatism of another era and a youth that was pro-Western and convinced it was at the dawn of a Renaissance. It was also as a political strategy, to avoid being absorbed by the new governing party. The difference between Fidesz and the MDF is clearly illustrated by Viktor Orbán's speech in Pécs in 1992: "The MDF represents an old and decadent world, which must never return to Hungary ... The hollow pathos of the governing parties, their beating about the bush as much as their crass chauvinism, is foreign to the spirit of Fidesz, since we spontaneously work to make the nation happy ... We don't think that general cultural values would have frustrated Hungarians' knowledge of their own national culture. We don't think we should be required to pursue our supposedly lost national consciousness all our lives, like King Arthur's knights in search of the Grail."[26] The MDF was a remnant of pre-war Hungary in its sclerotic forms, Fidesz an unprecedented version of eternal Hungary. Viktor Orbán went on to say: "Our generation is an obstacle to rebuilding the old, compromised world."

This detachment illustrates less a youthful insolence than a romantic temperament that was particularly keen in Hungary, where Reaction was one of the faces of foreign oppression.

Conservatism against Reaction

It is important to understand the evolution of Austrian guardianship in contemporary times. Napoleon's final defeat in 1815 was seen as a return to normality on the continent – and particularly in the Austrian Empire. But revolutionary excess gave rise to the opposite excess of reaction. The reactionary leaders sought as much as they could to erase the Revolution, even though it was part of an evolution whose beginnings had been evident throughout the continent even before 1789. Reaction can restore an old order but cannot resurrect its spirit.

The coalitionists had their minds elsewhere: an unshakeable reaction guaranteed their status as victorious powers. At the Congress of Vienna (1814-1815), Austria, Prussia, and Russia agreed to ensure the stability of the new European order. Vienna established itself as the guardian power of the German Confederation, the suzerain of Italy, and the undisputed mistress of Central Europe.

Prince Clemens von Metternich (1773-1859) dominated Viennese political life during this period. First as Foreign Minister from 1809, then

---

[26] Ibid, p. 111.

as Austria's Imperial Chancellor (1821-1848), he led a regime that was as tough as it was transient, since the empire had to set an example of unchanging order. Austria embraced the paradox between traditional intentions and effective modernity. As a modern state, it compressed subjugated countries in a patchwork under altar and throne. Its peoples became the sole object of the Austrian centralism once instituted to preserve them from the Ottoman peril. Paradoxically, Metternich, along with the other reactionary powers of Europe, now defended Turkish hegemony in the Balkans, fearing that Greek independence would give rise to national demands within his empire. For a time, the tone of the Hungarian nobility retained the accents of loyalty.[27]

The burden of the Holy Alliance falls mainly on "that heroic Poland on which the ingratitude of kings weighs."[28] During the revolutionary wave that swept across Europe in 1830, Austria did not lend a helping hand to neighboring Poland in the name of the Holy Alliance, even though Catholic sentiments argued in favor of such an arrangement. Failing to assimilate irremediable political fractures, Austria was exposed to the importation of innovations tried and tested in the west of the continent: national freedoms could only be regained through liberal provisions haloed by the prestige of France. In the stifling atmosphere of the winter of 1848, a revolutionary storm suddenly erupted in Paris and spread across the continent, known to history as the "Springtime of the Peoples."

In Buda, Sandor Petöfy declaimed his poem "Debout, Hongrois!" ("Stand Up Hungarians"), rallying the enthusiastic support of his audience: "Never again will we be slaves!" Led by Lajos Kossuth, the insurrection turns into a war of independence. Austria was forced to ask for help from the Russian army, which crossed the Carpathians in the spring of 1849. The respite granted to the Habsburgs by force would be swept away by force. In 1859, Austria lost its Italian possessions on the

---

[27] This protest from the Diet of the Comitat du Bars, sent to Emperor Francis I, bears witness to this: "We do not doubt that this rigorous censorship of our literature may appear useful to His Majesty's government. The ignorance of contemporary events that we owe to censorship perhaps makes the exercise of power easier. We only wonder whether virile minds can withstand such compression. What then are our sins? Why do we close before us the wellsprings of civilization? Why do we break the bonds of human society" (1815). cf. Louis Léger, *Histoire de l'Autriche-Hongrie*, 1879.

[28] The expression comes from Chateaubriand, *Mémoires d'outre-tombe*, Livre XII, 1849.

battlefields of Solferino and Magenta. Seven years later at Sadowa, Prussia's victory marked the beginning of German unity under the leadership of Berlin. The old imperial dream sank once and for all, as it was replaced by something else: the German and Italian nations.

Austria suffered a considerable loss of prestige, and the Reaction failed. A necessary internal recomposition followed. The Germans, a minority in the empire and excluded from the Germany Bismarck was building in the north, had to reconsider the very nature of the Austrian state. To do this, they needed a privileged interlocutor: Hungary. In 1867, bitter negotiations between Vienna and Budapest led to the re-foundation of the Austrian Empire as the Empire of Austria-Hungary. Cisleithania (the Austrian part) and Transleithania (the Hungarian part) recognized Franz Joseph I as sovereign: emperor in Austria and king in Hungary. On June 8, 1867, he was crowned in Budapest's St. Matthias Church. After 250 years of various forms of subjection, the Hungarians regained considerable autonomy in the countries of the Crown of St. Stephen. Austria regained its raison d'être rather than innovating. Instead of maintaining absolutist rule at arm's length, in the nineteenth century it adapted to new political circumstances to perpetuate the same destiny. From 1867 to 1918, the Austro-Hungarian Empire followed an alternative path to that of the ethnonational West. It was not Turkish or Russian otherness that had to be contained, but the unleashing of secessionist demands with no other goal than secession for national independence itself. Empire redefines the reciprocal obligations of neighbors whose isolation guarantees not freedom, but vulnerability.

*

Much water has flowed under the Danube's bridges since then. The wreckage of the imperial and communist eras has been succeeded by the era of the all-powerful market, in which Hungary intervenes as a national state. So it is not the same heavy-handedness that threatens to hamper the building of Hungary in the twenty-first century. The enthusiastic youth of Fidesz is confronted with the fatalism and inertia inherited from socialism. The reawakening of a conservative political consciousness in Hungary is due as much to the excesses of the new liberal system as to the skill of the opposing camp. Against this backdrop, the emergence of a civic-minded Hungary was Viktor Orbán's central preoccupation right up to the reshaping of the state in 2010.

*

While Orbán is keen to rid Hungary of old divisions, the same cannot be said of the advocates of liberal ideology, even those within the ranks of Fidesz. This trend is based on a segment of the population that is urban, well-to-do, and seduced by the American model at its height. It gives the impression that anti-communist dissidents were calling for the establishment of a new society based on the West's. This is a misinterpretation: some later rallied to this cause, but until 1990 all were groping for ways to widen their room for maneuver.[29]

In its embryonic stage, Fidesz saw itself as the party of youth, the only one capable of regenerating the whole of old Hungary, rusted through by socialism. It experimented with a "neither right nor left" approach, but this aspiration to transcend the divide[30] came up against the country's long-standing political polarization. The liberal Alliance of Free Democrats (SzDSz) colluded with the socialists (Hungarian Socialist Party - MSZP), i.e. the left inherited from the communist regime, and urged Fidesz to join the "progressive" camp. In autumn 1991, a "Democratic Charter" was submitted to all political parties to unite the opposition. Fidesz signed up in good faith, but it was in fact an attempt by the communists to re-emerge as the herald of any struggle against reaction. The moral authority of the left was certainly not recognized by the anti-communist youth of Fidesz, but the ambition to draw certain valid tendencies from the left was maintained for several years. Gabor Fodor, Orbán's friend from the military and university, became the leader of this trend.

Between 1990 and 1993, the attempt to create a national synthesis of

---

[29] Confirmation of this approach can be found in the words of a Fidesz co-founder, Laszlo Köver, to journalist Amélie Poinssot: "After fifty years of communism, the traditional categories of left/right, Christian democracy and liberalism no longer had the same meaning in Hungary. In the face of absolute power, fighting for the right to freedom was considered liberalism. We accepted this concept as such. » *Dans la tête de Viktor Orbán*, Actes Sud, 2018.

[30] This consensual project was inspired by the work of Istvan Bibo, a Hungarian minister who fell in 1956.

liberals and conservatives united by good will came to nothing. Young Hungarians were derided for their centrism: they sought the "Belgian way" (so as not to have to choose between Flanders and Wallonia); they were called children of divorced parents. Orbán gradually realized that the only way to build an independent political force was to break with the liberal galaxy. At the end of these years of trial and error, a major political lesson was learned: the divide proved insurmountable. Although they shared a common language and institutions, two nations coexisted in Hungary. These are the two poles around which the country's political life is organized. In the spring of 1993, the Hungarian-born American billionaire George Soros invited Orbán, Laszlo Köver, and Klara Ungar, a close associate of Fodor, to lunch. The billionaire depicted the Western world as a diptych of liberals and cryptofascists. It is important, he says, for Fidesz to ally itself with the liberals and socialists, which Orbán flatly refused to do.[31]

Orbán's detractors accuse him of having chosen his political camp more out of pragmatism than conviction. In a sense, that is true: an ideological hat does not suit him. The national cause that matters to him is both irreducible to theory and subject to infinitely varied circumstances, such as the ascendancy of globalist logics. The socialists and liberals were in the service of international finance capital, an option that was neither socially responsible nor favorable to Hungarian freedoms. Fidesz's "right-wing" stance is therefore the result of political adversity.

A party of national interest

Viktor Orbán was elected president of Fidesz at the Debrecen congress in April 1993. Whereas Gabor Fodor wanted to calm conflicts, Viktor Orbán wanted to resolve them – and win. In his victory speech, Orbán asserted the need to take a "national-liberal" path. Fidesz's turn to the right dates from this period. Gabor Fodor was ousted from the promised presidency of the National Committee in favor of the Orbánist József Szajer; ties were strengthened with Zsolt Bayer, an eternal fellow traveler and today one of the most influential personalities on the Hungarian media scene.

---

[31] Ibid, p. 134.

Following the Debrecen Congress, Orbán, at the age of 30, experienced an all-out war waged against him by the press: *Nepszabadsag*, a liberal, formerly communist newspaper that had hitherto gone easy on Fidesz began a merciless campaign on May 24, 1993. The aim was to denounce its national-populist turn and to accuse Fidesz of corruption and of having compromised with the ruling MDF. Corruption was suspected in connection with a former casino that had been converted into the party's headquarters and alleged VAT fraud.

The Hungarian urban class had little sympathy for the party's conservative tendencies, and Fodor's criticism of his former comrade went from strength to strength, making him more popular than Orbán, even though he was sidelined in the party, which he left in November 1993. While Orbán found himself isolated and powerless in the face of the unexpected and combined hostility of opinion leaders, his relations with Prime Minister Antall improved. Negotiations with the MDF, in power but in disarray, paved the way for a major conservative platform for the 1994 elections. When Antall died prematurely on December 12, 1993, Orbán honored in him a predecessor, but was under no illusions about the limits of this political experiment. In four years, the Conservatives had failed to establish anything lasting. The machinery of state remained in the hands of communist-era elites, an anachronism in a rapidly changing international context. Hungary had emerged from communism into an interregnum.

*

The difficulties of the post-socialist transition explain the pendulum swing in the 1994 elections. Fidesz fell to just 7% of the vote. Victory went to the former communists (MSZP) with 33%, followed by the Liberals (SzDSz) with 19.7%. These two parties formed a strong coalition, to the great satisfaction of the liberal West. Their alliance attested to the compatibility of the two foreign-inspired dynamics. As Orbán concluded, "Birds of a feather flock together." In his eyes, a crypto-communist Hungary remained at the helm despite the emergence of a civic-minded Hungary.

Orbán conceded defeat and put his party's presidency back on the line.

Reappointed, he built Fidesz into a power-grabbing machine. In 1995, the party presented a coalition program with the MDF. The party changed its name to Fidesz Magyar Polgári Párt (Hungarian Civic Party). From 1994, the various right-wing parties began to come together on the basis of national traditions and Christian democracy. Fidesz's doctrinal content was already moving away from the liberal economic catechism: "Hungary does not simply need modernization. As quickly as possible, we want to see the introduction of an economic policy that guarantees an expansion of the middle class, whose prosperity is growing in Hungary. It is a given that the unbridled market cannot put an end to the economic stagnation."

*

In the eyes of the conservative side, Viktor Orbán's transformation into the leader of their sensibility is first and foremost suspect. He could not be more conservative, in the narrow sense of the term, than the MDF, no more Christian than the KDNP (Christian Democratic People's Party), and no more populist than the FKgP (Independent Civic Party of Smallholders and Agrarian Workers).

It was up to Fidesz to breathe new political vitality into these elements, which would materialize through the blossoming of the middle class. Viktor Orbán's spearhead ideal was "civicmindedness," a notion that overcomes the divisions on the Hungarian right. The "Polgár" (citizen) has become a key idea. The role of the state is to help those who help themselves, those who honor their civic responsibilities.

At the same time, neoliberal policies were eroding the left-wing government's popularity. Fidesz protested against the burden placed on the middle class. It criticized the government for following economic policies recommended by international institutions: "the government must represent our interests to the IMF, not the other way around." A critique of the economic model imposed on Central Europe since 1990 was emerging. Foreign direct investment (FDI), celebrated by liberal orthodoxy, caused concern, as conservatives saw it as a double-edged sword: a short-term boon for the Hungarian economy, but also a vector of lasting dispossession.

Fidesz was not content to simply reach out to the traditional pre-World

War II middle class. It is also concerned with the communist-era middle class, adrift under the *laissez faire* approach of the liberal-socialist coalition. The latter openly wielded power for the benefit of the large-scale, mainly foreign, economic players.

*

To succeed, Orbán's path required considerable reinforcements. Various players were organizing the intellectual consolidation of Fidesz, including the Századvég Foundation, which was tasked with providing reports and analyses for the conquest of power two years later. Another group, headed by András Wermer, was responsible for electoral strategy. A veterans' council (Vének Tanácsa) provides training for Viktor Orbán, meeting weekly from 9pm until very late at night. János Horváth, the dean of the Hungarian Parliament at the time, remembers the young MP's passionate curiosity: this was more than just political coaching.

For Viktor Orbán, the 1998 elections represented a huge challenge: the validation of the political direction he imposed on an undecided right or a complete loss of credibility after eight years in opposition. The poor results of the outgoing government were mitigated by media indulgence; conversely, the consistency of the conservatives' political program was hardly perceptible to the majority. It was Orbán's personality and popular background that most eloquently defended his political line.

The socialists' main campaign argument was that there was no alternative, whereas Fidesz dwelled neither on the past (communism, from which all but a few die-hard activists had fled) nor on the present (the scandals that marred four years of leftist coalition government): entirely on the task that awaits the country. Fidesz agreed with what was honorable about the communist era, notably the possibility for everyone to have a job, a policy that Fidesz hoped to preserve, Orbán citing his own family as an example. Civic dynamism is strikingly innovative: Fidesz did not change society, it changes itself. Citizens are the actors of national life, building a country worthy of their merit, something no government can do for them: "Circumstances do not shape the world. It is the will of the people." In this sense, democracy is the participation of a people in its own destiny; not the art of defending the people, but the people's art of defending themselves. The choice is not between two parties, but between two political concepts. Orbán has never hesitated to draw a line: "One lacks credibility, is lazy and degraded, the other is characterized by proactivity and pride."

On May 20, the debate between the two main candidates took place at the Budapest University of Economics: the socialist Gyula Horn (outgoing Prime Minister) and the conservative Viktor Orbán; a 66-year old former communist facing a young conservative of 35. The contest went clearly in the latter's favor. Accused by his opponent of defending the bourgeoisie through the figure of the "Polgár" (indeed, this is one of the definitions in Hungarian), Orbán retorted that he only has dictionaries from the Communist era before expatiating about his vision of civicmindedness. This alternative to stale leftist statism proved an alternative both demanding and seductive to the Hungarian people.

*

Victory came on May 24, 1998. Fidesz grew from 22 to 148 deputies and took the lead of a conservative coalition reinforced by the MDF and the FKgP. The team forged by the anti-communist dissident movement of the 1980s formed Orbán's bodyguard ten years later, with the loyal Laszlo Köver serving as minister without portfolio in charge of the secret services.

The traditional character of Orbán's politics was already apparent at this time. He adopted the maxim of a famous nineteenth-century Hungarian, Count István Széchenyi (1791-1860): "We must dare to be great." In his time, this important national figure contributed to Hungary's modernization. Founder of the Academy of Sciences in 1825, the Count made considerable efforts to drain the Tisza marshes. From one century to the next, the ambition was similar: to restore Hungary's grandeur, to be something other than a poor periphery of the Germanic world, whether as part of the Austrian Empire or the European Union.

In the past, England was the model of efficiency to be imitated; in the twenty-first century, Hungarians are not afraid to turn their gaze inward. Regaining greatness requires the development of a domestic market and the mobilization of the middle class as the country's economic engine. The mirage of foreign investment is dissipating in the face of a determination *hic et nunc* to build on local entrepreneurship. The government is combining lower taxation with reductions in the public deficit.

In four years of government, 12,000 new homes were built and 46,000 new jobs created. Industrial production grew by 23%. National companies were favored in the awarding of public contracts. When Austrian diplomats complained that their companies were being squeezed out and asked the Budapest government when they could expect to win public works contracts, Orbán replied: "when Hungarian companies win public contracts in Austria."

Despite a few national principles of political economy, Orbán's only ambition at the time was to integrate Hungary into the capitalist West. He clearly retained the Western tropism of his anti-communist youth. The prospect of EU and NATO membership seemed an unavoidable horizon given the legacy of communism and the benefits of pro-Western integration.

On the other hand, the government's national consciousness produced its first sparks. In 2000, the Hungarian state celebrated its thousandth anniversary. The millennium was celebrated in every Hungarian village. At the same time, the House of Terror museum inaugurated in Budapest underlined the wholesale rejection of the deadly ideologies of the twentieth century, with communism and Nazism both turned on their heads. Hungary was forging ahead, unwavering in its destiny.

IV.

The school of adversity

Modern experiences

At the turn of the millennium, Fidesz's software still lacked a key element: resilience to hostility, both domestically and internationally. Mimicry of the Western system inhibited this identification of the civic nation with itself: Hungary lacked consistency. Its relationship with the EU was characterized by a candid amity. Setbacks soon played a decisive role in shaping the new Hungarian model suddenly established in 2010.

The liberal stagnation in Central Europe was all the more rapid because it prolonged a century of vicissitudes. Since the Great War, the Visegrád countries had gone from disappointment to failure. Emancipation was heralded in 1918, when Czech deputies issued the following declaration in Paris:

> Our nation claims its independence. It relies on its historic right of statehood and is fully imbued with the desire to be able, in emulation with free nations, to contribute in a sovereign and democratic state, comprising its historic countries and its Slovak offshoot, to the new development of humanity, which will be based on freedom and fraternity. In this state, the Czech nation will grant full and equal rights to national minorities. We ask that all nations, including our own, be given the opportunity to take part in the Peace Congress and to defend their rights there in complete freedom.[32]

The deprivations of war made the cup overflow. And yet, after the continual dismantling of custom in the nineteenth century, imperfect or

---

[32] Czech parliamentarians' Epiphany declaration, January 6, 1918.

incomplete historical rights were a virtual guarantee. Their liquidation proved to be an immense loss, for the false privilege of being a people like any other at a time of totalitarian ideologies. Admittedly, Bohemia gained nominal sovereignty and territorial gains with the formation of Czechoslovakia. But the decades that followed showed just how versatile the right of peoples to self-determination could be, serving the interests of the strongest. Twenty years later, the Germans seized hegemony over Czechoslovakia, when the West stooped to sign the Munich Agreement,[33] and then unilaterally dissolved and occupied the rump Czech lands. as the "Protectorate of Bohemia-Moravia," an autonomous unit within the Reich, with its own administration under a Nazi official. Between 1938 and 1948, Czechoslovakia passed through occupation, war and liberation – from the Nazi to the Soviet fold – for four long decades with true independence a fleeting dream. In 1990, compared to 1920, the country had fallen from tenth to fortieth place among the world's industrial powers.[34] The loss represented by the felling of the Habsburg oak can be measured.

Hungary was under no illusions. In the immediate post-war period, it was subjected to a communist dictatorship[35] with far less pretense to democracy than the Czechs enjoyed, but above all, on June 4, 1920, it signed the Treaty of Trianon, which confirmed its defeat in the First World War in the worst possible way. Two-thirds of Hungary's territory was taken away, and 3.3 million Hungarians found themselves living abroad (in Austria, Romania, Czechoslovakia, and Yugoslavia).

By contrast, 1918 saw the resurrection of the Polish state, with borders approaching those before the partitions of the eighteenth century. Marshal Józef Piłsudski (1867-1935) stopped the Bolsheviks at the gates of Warsaw and built the Second Republic, but failed to resolve the territorial dispute with Germany before his death. In the ethnocultural checkerboard of Europe at the time, a unitary state could only assert itself at the expense of other peoples.

From 1914 to 1945, an infernal spiral trapped the Old Continent between Charybdis and Scylla. The countries of Central Europe were

---

[33] September 30, 1938.
[34] Antoine Marès, *Histoire des Tchèques et des Slovaques*, Perrin, 2005.
[35] The Republic of Councils, March to August 1919.

traditionally multi-ethnic. There were many Germans in Bohemia and Moravia; many Germans, Belarusians, and Ukrainians in Poland; Germans again, Slavs of different nationalities, and Romanians in Hungary; Hungarians in the countries mentioned; and Jews in every country. This human geography seemed no less immutable than the physical one. The "Thirty Years' War" of the twentieth century (1914-1945) turned this landscape upside down. At Yalta in February 1945, the USSR, the United States, and the United Kingdom – the major World War II Allied powers – decided to establish ethnonationalism in Central Europe, reorganizing borders and displacing populations. Winston Churchill spoke before the House of Commons of the need to redefine Central Europe according to the model of "one country, one people." In two phases, 1918 and 1945, the Visegrád countries forcibly entered the ethnonational era. The major phenomenon was the expulsion from 1945 of ten million Germans from lands where they had lived since the Middle Ages. The German-Polish border now followed the Oder-Neisse line. The result of German nationalism turned out to be the scuttling of the Germanic presence in Mitteleuropa, just as France had undermined the European pre-eminence of its culture through revolutionary imperialism. A century apart, the continent's two main powers lost Europe to the mirage of an exclusive nation. Today, German influence is making a comeback through European integration. But is it like a river momentarily diverted and finding its way back to its bed, or like the movement of anonymous capital in a soulless economy?

Reasons for defeat

When Fidesz took the helm of state in 1998, it accepted the twentieth century's burdensome liabilities without a second thought. The aim was to bring the country into this seemingly inescapable framework, while protecting its vital interests. Viktor Orbán's first government represented a four-year incision in power after sixteen years in opposition.

The Fidesz government faced a challenging environment at home and abroad. Most of the machinery of power lay in the hands of former communists who had never really left positions of responsibility and regained the ascendancy in post-communist institutions during the previous mandate (1994-1998). The minutes of the first ministerial meetings found their way into the press: the cleaning ladies emptied the office bins on behalf of the Socialist Party. Officials' government cars broke down at the instigation of the department in charge of their maintenance.[36]

In 2002, many Hungarians had yet to benefit from the Orbán administration. Attacks from those nostalgic for the communist era and from the progressives converged, abundantly relayed by the compliant media. The dynamism of Fidesz offended a section of the population accustomed to the inertia of socialism. Orbán cultivated a combative style that did him a disservice in the eyes of some. His opponents described him as an autocrat; the nickname "Viktator" was already in circulation and suspicions of democratic usurpation spread. The dominant press denounced the growing power of the Fidesz business community and Lajos Simicska's allied media group.

Nevertheless, the 2002 campaign got off to a good start. EU membership was scheduled for 2004, with the expected structural funds, and a new mandate was needed to complete the Széchenyi Plan. Fidesz highlighted the work that has been done, including the construction of considerable infrastructure. The Socialists campaigned under the slogan "Hungary deserves better:" recent successes were said to be due to the general economic situation, while negative resulted were attributed to Orbán's government. Advised by top-flight foreign marketing teams, the Socialists adjusted their political promises according to the views of the electorate they were targeting. They promised to raise pension levels and return to "normality" after four tumultuous years.

In 2000, Viktor Orbán left the presidency of his party to devote himself entirely to the exercise of power, so he remained in the background during the campaign. His record was supposed to ensure victory. In contrast to his duel with Gyula Horn four years earlier, the debate with the socialist Péter Medgyessy did not go his way. Finally, on April 17, 2002, Fidesz obtained a disappointing score. Despite strong mobilization in the run-up to the elections, the April 21 vote failed to reverse the trend. Fidesz remained the country's largest party but was unable to secure a

---

[36] Hungarian European Commissioner, member of the Juncker Commission (2014-2019).

conservative majority in Parliament. The Socialists and Liberals sent Orbán back into opposition. He remained there for eight years.

*

The former Prime Minister realized the mistake he had made in relinquishing the party leadership and took matters into his own hands. On May 7, 2002, he called for the foundation of "civic circles" to discuss not ideological controversies, but what citizens can do for themselves. Csaba Hende, the first coordinator of this initiative, explained that the social dynamism crushed by communism was never restored. According to him, pre-war Hungary was like a fishbowl that the socialist regime turned into fish soup. Fidesz's objective in opposition was "to turn a fish soup into an aquarium in which we can swim freely." Fidesz rolled up its sleeves: while it had lost power, it planted deeper roots in civil society. Through the subsequent absorption of civic circles, Orbán renewed and expanded Fidesz. During his eight years in opposition, Fidesz grew from 5,000 to 30,000 members, making it the most organized and influential party in Central Europe. The work of repoliticizing society gave citizens the means to express themselves and be heard.

In March 2004, Fidesz launched a major petition calling for the restoration of housing benefits, a reduction in the price of medicine, a halt to the privatization of hospitals and privatizations in general, a limit in gasoline price increases to 5% a year, and an increase in farm subsidies. Building a national system was the objective. The hand extended to the modest heirs of late communism was confirmed by the promotion of Pál Schmitt, a great sportsman of the communist era and Secretary General of the Hungarian Olympic Committee, to the post of Vice-President of Fidesz.

Orbán did not rest still in opposition. Defeat did not lock him into bitterness, but rather multiplied his thirst for enterprise. A keen football fan, in 2007 he inaugurated a soccer academy, the Puskás Ferenc Academy, in his village of Felcsút. The former Prime Minister was responsible for rallying the major companies OTP and MOL to finance the project. He also called on Imre Makovecz, a leader in organic architecture, to bring an aesthetic dimension to the infrastructures erected to the glory of Hungarian soccer.

*

In May 2004, Fidesz won Hungary's first balloting in European elections with 47% of the vote. This result led to a cabinet reshuffle and the appointment of Ferenc Gyurcsány as Prime Minister, a post he held until 2009. It was in Ferenc Gyurcsány that Viktor Orbán found his most formidable political adversary. They disagreed on everything, starting with their social predilections. The new prime minister was infatuated with the upper middle class, the other with the working-class, provincial Hungarians. In a 1989 recording, the young Fidesz spokesman referred to his future opponent as the only KISZ executive[37] to be taken seriously. The transition to a market economy worked wonders for the ambitious Ferenc Gyurcsány: he turned to finance, where he achieved remarkable success and soon became one of the fifty richest people in the country. He returned to politics in earnest in 2002, serving as Minister of Children, Youth, and Sport in the Medgyessy government.

The Gyurcsány-Orbán duel was immediately vituperative. Shortly after his appointment, the new Prime Minister granted an interview to the various political party leaders. When Orbán arrived at his office door, where numerous journalists had congregated to cover the event, he was made to wait interminably for the head of government to deign to open the door. The humiliation was stinging.

In the run-up to the 2006 parliamentary elections, Fidesz attacked the achievements of the government with the slogan "The situation is worse than four years ago." The traditional debate turned into a disaster for Orbán. Assured of dominating his opponent by confronting him with a disappointing record, he found himself unprepared for the socialist's caustic assurances. Fidesz and MSZP still finished neck and neck, with 42% and 43%, respectively, but the MDF obtained less than the Liberals and also distanced itself from Orbán. The latter then gave up his claim to be Prime Minister in order to retain the MDF alliance in the second round. Fidesz voters were disoriented, and their turnout waned. Against all expectations, after a very mixed experience, the liberal-socialist incumbents were re-elected and the right plunged into divisions.

---

[37] After the fall of the socialist regime, Ferenc Gyurcsány became vice-president of DEMISZ, KISZ's legal successor.

While the conservative camp was moping about, it was a carefree time: the inevitable financial collapse of 2008 was not even suspected. In other words, while the liberal conscience was eating its cake, Orbán was forced to retreat and develop a resilience whose scope is now clear to see.

Political vulnerability in Central Europe

Even when left to their own devices, recent or long-defunct political structures carry a high risk of failure. This difficulty affects all the countries of Central Europe. This assertion calls for a brief presentation of Slovak history.

In the eighth century, the short-lived Kingdom of Samo, centered in present-day Moravia, included the Slavic tribes that would one day form the Czech Republic and Slovakia. At the time of the Magyar conquest, Slavic peasants lived in the valleys of the Tatras, a mountain range stretching from west to east and forming the northern part of the Carpathian basin. As fortune would have it, these mountains fell within the Hungarian orbit rather than that of Poland. A thousand years of subordination did not led to the assimilation of the Slovaks. Deprived of political rights that were the prerogative of the nobility alone, the peasants of Upper Hungary remained subjects of the kingdom. Slovakia illustrates the fragile incubation of one nation within another. The beginnings of an awakening identity could be observed under the reign of Joseph II (1780-1790), notably following the abolition of serfdom in 1785. The Viennese centralism that prevailed at the time led to the abandonment of Latin as the official language in Hungary, in favor of German. The attempt to Germanize Hungary led to the subsequent Magyarization of administrative, judicial, and religious domains throughout the Kingdom of St. Stephen. The Slovak language gained popularity, as evidenced by its first codification in 1787, and enabled Slavs in Upper Hungary to assert themselves as Slovaks. From the colleges of Bratislava, then called Pozsony in Hungarian and Pressburg in German, emerged defenders of the language and culture of the mountain people of northern Hungary. The proximity of the Czech neighbor offered Slovaks the prospect of a different future.

After the First World War, Slovakia became part of Czechoslovakia.

As in Yugoslavia, the country's constituent parts were determined to pull out all the stops. The Ruthenians and Slovaks served first and foremost as a counterweight to wealthy Bohemia, just as the Croats and Slovenes in the south served as a counterweight to ambitious Serbia. Slovakia's first "independence" – in reality a German protectorate – resulted from the dismantling of Czechoslovakia by Germany in 1938. The newly independent country promptly ceded its Magyar-speaking southern fringe back to Hungary, under the terms of the first Vienna Arbitration. This arrangement was reversed at the end of the war, with the resurrection of Czechoslovakia under Soviet domination. On January 1, 1993, however, Prague and Bratislava amicably agreed to separate in the so-called "Velvet Divorce." Slovakia has thus known only thirty years of true independence.

History has not allowed Slovakia to acquire a sense of statehood and political culture through a national elite. As a result, it is largely determined by the outside world, whether Brussels or its Visegrád neighbors. Bratislava, located on the Austrian border, is strongly under German influence, and the country's adoption of the euro has deprived this capital-starved economy of much room for maneuver. Hungarians on the southern edge of the country turn to Budapest, while the dynamism of Poland and the Czech Republic is a strong attraction in the north and west.

Slovakia's identity is emblematic of an era of widespread political dispossession. World maps are deceptive. In fact, from the Balkans to the Baltic, many of Europe's smaller countries have no politics other than that of the dominant power of the day. A comparison of Hungary and Romania proves that size is not the only element of political consistency. Although twice as populous and boasting a coastline, Romania's policies are largely dependent on the prevailing winds and the country's adjustment proved much slower. But Romania is distinguished by a singular, vibrant culture, and it is this deep-rootedness that ultimately enables it to defy the centuries and empires.

The end of the tunnel

September 17, 2006. Suddenly, the situation was turned upside down.

Hungarian radio made public a recording of confidential remarks by Ferenc Gyurcsány the previous May, at a meeting of elected members of his new majority:

> We no longer have a choice. Not because we screwed up ... Not a little, but totally. No European country has screwed up as badly as we have. Obviously, we've been lying for the last eighteen months. It was perfectly clear that what we were saying was not true. We've done nothing for four years, nothing. You can't name a single significant measure we can be proud of, apart from the fact that we got ourselves out of trouble in the end.

The outcry was immense. Viktor Orbán, who was in Brussels at the time, told the opposition not to get carried away, while a wave of indignation led to rallies calling for the resignation of the government. It is possible that the publication of the recording was not accidental. State malpractice during the Gyurcsány era had become so widespread that drastic reforms had to be made at some point. The disguised public accounts presented to the European Commission placed the head of the Hungarian government under international pressure. Between a public confession and the orchestrated leak of a recording, Gyurcsány would have likely preferred the second option. As for the violence committed at the demonstrations, it is not impossible that the powers-that-be were trying to use it to delegitimize popular anger while at the same time setting themselves up as a bulwark against the furious far right.

The scandal did not abate and calls for Gyurcsány's resignation continued throughout the autumn. Demonstrations by the radical right were filmed by the pro-Fidesz Hir television channel. Opposition media became fashionable, and nationalists made their mark on the political landscape under the banner of the Jobbik party. Conservative and radical right-wingers found a large popular audience.

It was in this context of unexpected political recomposition that the commemorations of the fiftieth anniversary of the Budapest uprising were prepared. Half a century earlier, the socialists' predecessors in power had been accomplices in Soviet repression. Communism, the Left, the party of the foreigner and incompetence all merged into one disgraced face: that of Ferenc Gyurcsány.

Far from eclipsing partisan quarrels, the commemorations of the uprising of October 23, 1956 rekindled memories of anti-Soviet resistance. Ferenc Gyurcsány was humiliated by the audience, who turn their backs on him as he vainly attempted to interact with the crowd. An afternoon demonstration degenerated into violence. Police repression, water cannons, and tear gas gave the day a particularly evocative air of insurrection.[38] These events crystalized the discontent of Hungarians under a long-awaited post-communist period that painfully resembled an interregnum. A realization transfigured society: the nation had gone astray, it had not been restored to itself in 1990 so it vegetated in a deleterious sloppiness, under the sway of foreign principles incapable of breathing new life into it.

*

Whole swathes of the electorate turned away from the left-wing parties, leading not only to the strengthening of Fidesz, but also to the assertiveness of Jobbik, to the right of Fidesz. The conservatives fleshed out their program in order to assert themselves in the general reshaping of Hungarian political life. Orbán worked hard and surrounded himself with remarkably qualified teams. Tibor Navracsics, leader of the Fidesz group in Parliament, established himself as a leading figure in the chamber, contributing to the intellectual aura of the conservative opposition. He organized a series of debates entitled "Our future – on the condition of our country." Discussions focused on justice, quality of life, competitiveness, and public services. These debates led to the adoption of the "Our Future" program in May 2007.

Fidesz organized petitions and demonstrations on the occasion of a reform of the healthcare system, attracting a large number of people beyond the party. In March 2008, the collection of signatures led to the organization of a referendum on three themes: the cost of medical consultations, the daily cost of hospital care, and the cost of education.

---

[38] A full report on "Hungary's Other Revolution" was produced in 2016 by Nicolas de Lamberterie for the *TVLibertés* channel: https://www.tvlibertes.com/2006-lautre-revolution-hongroise-az-elveszett-forradalom

Some 82% of voters rejected the government's proposals. In the run-up to the elections, the political groundwork was laid for the historic rematch of 2010.

The 2008 crisis hit the Hungarian economy hard. A Greek-style scenario of high debt loomed. The executive appealed to the IMF for a loan. In 2009, the Socialists, abandoned by the Liberals, found themselves unable to form a government. Ferenc Gyurcsány, who had lost even the indulgence of the Western media, was forced to resign, giving way to Gordon Bajnai to form a minority government until the 2010 elections. By 2009,[39] it seemed certain that Fidesz would take power. Orbán worked to strengthen his position in the party as his aura grew across the country.

On April 11, 2010, the Fidesz-led alliance won 52.7% of the vote in the first round. Two weeks later, it won a two-thirds majority in Parliament (263 seats out of 386). Viktor Orbán confided to *Frankfurter Allgemeine Zeitung* that he would "like to take credit for the destruction of the left in Hungary, but the left has actually committed suicide."

---

[39] In May 2009, Fidesz won Hungary's European elections with over 56% of the vote.

V.

The peaceful revolution

Rebuilding a sovereign state

In Viktor Orbán's eyes, the status quo regime could not be reformed, but had to be overthrown. He intended to replace the opaque grip of the socialist elite with a "system of national cooperation."[40] His constitutional majority accorded him such an opportunity. "The new Parliament is more than just the sixth parliament that emerged from Hungary's free elections. The new assembly was in reality a constituent national assembly and a founding parliament of a new system."[41] A veritable conservative revolution was taking place within the European Union, which has ratified the Lisbon Treaty. Under the 2010-2014 legislature, Fidesz reorganized the State to make it a political instrument at the service of the nation, a platform that has enabled Hungary to play a role on the European stage disproportionate to its size.

The peaceful restoration of thousand-year-old Hungary made history on April 18, 2011, with the adoption of the new constitution. The country's official name became *Magyarország* (Hungary), replacing *Magyar köztársaság* (Republic of Hungary). Above all, this fundamental law placed the new regime within the continuity of previous centuries. The preamble mentions the Holy Crown as the symbol of state continuity and national unity, enshrines the family and the nation as essential frameworks of community life, and honors work as the foundation of human dignity.

The desire to reconnect with the country's fundamental identity

---

[40] Nemzeti Együttműködés Rendszere (NER); the acronym is now in common use in Hungary. In turn, the opposition denounces an opaque and corrupt system.
[41] From the political program presented to Parliament.

explains the path taken by Viktor Orbán in terms of religion.[42] Unlike in Poland, the Hungarian Church served the communist authorities, and the rebellious youth behind Fidesz had little regard for the episcopate. During the socialist era, two events marked the youthful dissident. The spiritual dimension of the Polish Solidarność movement and his marriage in 1986 to Anikó Lévai, a devout Catholic. Fidesz's reconciliation with religion dates back to 1992. Orbán became aware of the support he could find there: "I had no idea that the Church was so important in Hungary, and how much it counts in people's lives. I can't act properly in politics if I miss out on that." After first coming to power in 1998, the young head of government made his first official trip to the Vatican. The heart of the matter was neither dogma (Viktor Orbán is a Calvinist) nor religious practice. Orbán relies on a patrimonial Christianity to animate a thousand years of historical continuity and exalt the country's unity. This is as much an effort to spiritually ennoble the age[43] as it is an intimate preoccupation of deep personal conviction.

The era of the "Hungarian People's Republic" was definitively over and entered the annals of history as a period of occupation that must be laid to rest. Such a version denigrates the MSZP as an agent from abroad: the war between the two Hungaries continues – so much so that Fidesz has learned its lessons of the exclusive behavior of its adversaries.

A raft of rapidly adopted laws facilitated the gradual sidelining of the former Communist elite. The retirement age for judges was lowered from 70 to 62.[44] The aim was to remove certain incompetent judges, but above all those with ties to the previous regime.

The Magyar-speaking populations of neighboring countries were not

---

[42] The words of József Szájer illustrate this connection: "Politics goes hand in hand with the emotions that hold the members of a society together. It's in this perspective that we need to understand our return to religion. In Europe, as in Hungary, today's parties are becoming too rational. They put emotions aside, they no longer talk about the nationality of their voters. Yet it's not with a policy of social redistribution that people identify, but with the history of their country!" cf. *Dans la tête de Victor Orbán*, Amélie Poinssot, Actes Sud, 2018.

[43] "A Christian Democrat policy means defending the forms of existence that stem from Christian culture. Not articles of faith, but ways of life that stem from them: the dignity of man, the family, the nation." Viktor Orbán, Tusványos speech, 2018.

[44] A subsequent agreement increased the retirement age to 65 but excluded any position of authority after 62.

only offered dual nationality upon request, but can also vote in parliamentary elections using the new single-round voting system. The 199 deputies of the unicameral Parliament are now elected, 106 of them in the country's constituencies, and the remaining 93 by proportional representation on the lists of the various competing parties. Hungarians from the Carpathian region abroad can take part in this list voting. Solidarity with the Hungarian population, lost since the Treaty of Trianon, is as much a part of Fidesz's original intentions as the defense of the family, individual responsibility and democracy.

Viktor Orbán took over the reins of a country with no appreciable army or energy resources, colonized in many respects, with 2% of the European Union's population and 0.8% of its GDP. These obvious limitations explained the adjustments he then made. Thus, the desire to reduce the Hungarian Central Bank's independence from national representation came to nothing, until a more propitious opportunity presented itself.

*

Major political reforms were spread over two years. But the government's first priority was to tackle the economic depression. To finance his program, Orbán pushed through emergency taxes on four sectors: banking and insurance, energy, telecommunications, and retail sales. These sectors were in the hands of foreign companies and generated large surpluses on the back of Hungarian labor. As the tax applied to profits, i.e. the bonuses of the richest, the ideological vindictiveness of the "no borders" left was compounded by the anger of overlapping Western business circles. The Hungarian government also decided to nationalize three trillion forints[45] from private pension funds to shore up the budget. The payment of these pensions is now the responsibility of the state. This *coup de force* meant that the budget for family policies – a priority if society is to plan for the future – would not be cut too much. Tax relief for families and small businesses was matched by a three-year increase in the retirement age. A reduction in the number of civil servants cut of fifteen government ministries to eight attested to further efficient management of

---

[45] About eleven billion euros

public funds. The country is recovered from the 2008 crisis and completed its IMF debt repayment early, in August 2013.

The Hungarian government's heterodox economic policy came under immediate attack from the opposition and Brussels. Accused of betraying the fundamentals of capitalism, Viktor Orbán retorted that he was simply building a national economy capable of participating viably in the European economy. The Hungarian model is a compromise, compatible with the German ordo-liberalism imposed by European competition and regulations across the continent. The exaltation of the nation and the value of work were put to use in the service of an economy integrated into the EU. But reciprocally, economic growth serves public power and allows for greater political leeway in the service of national independence.

*

When it came to power, the MDF was only willing to support conservative media. Viktor Orbán judged this wait-and-see attitude harshly: "The fact that a right-wing government came to power after 40 years of socialism was a gift from history. Not knowing how to make the most of this opportunity was beyond redemption." The media remain largely the preserve of an urban, intellectual left. Heirs to the communist era, they deplored the supposed infringement of freedom of expression when the right publishes a newspaper. In the early 1990s, only 6% of journalists at (Magyar Újságírók Országos Szövetsége) supported József Antall's conservative government. Fidesz, on the other hand, was in vogue: 38% of journalists claimed to be Fidesz supporters, with 13% for the Socialists and 12% for the Liberals. By 2000, Fidesz had moved to the right: 29% of journalists supported the Socialists, 24% the liberals and 22% the three-party coalition in government, including Fidesz.

A business community has been sorely lacking in the party's media presence. Fidesz treasurer Lajos Simicska took up the challenge. The weekly Heti Válasz was born in 2001; Hir TV was founded in 2002. These pioneering media were joined by the daily Magyar Hírlap, bought in 2005 by businessman Gábor Széles, and the Echo TV channel, also founded in 2005.

Back in power in 2002, the Socialists were openly hostile to right-wing media. Some outlets went under, and numerous resignations illustrated the Hungarian media's spoils system. Ferenc Gyurcsány refused to grant an interview to *Magyar Nemzet* or any like-minded newspaper. In an official letter, the head of government advised state-owned companies not to advertise in right-wing newspapers. The situation was reversed in 2010. Even the left-leaning public broadcaster, Lánchíd Radio, Magyar Demokrata, and other media outlets were strengthening the conservative camp. Clearly, the Hungarian media is politicized. But unlike the situation in Western Europe, they are not all in the same boat. Press trends illustrate the political and economic power relations at work in the country.

Competition is not without its rules. Established in 2010, the Media Council (Médiatanács) oversees press freedom, replacing the old system, which was rife with corruption and nepotism. The new institution is similar to France's Conseil supérieur de l'audiovisuel (CSA).[46] The president is appointed by Parliament for a nine-year term. The institution ensures fair treatment of news and respect for human dignity. Since 2010, and the current situation[47] has confirmed the plurality and freedom of information that prevail in Hungary.

Asserting ourselves on the international stage

Relations between Viktor Orbán and Brussels first came into conflict when Hungary took over the rotating EU presidency in the first half of 2011. Liberal media vindictiveness was unleashed, notably because of new legislation governing the press. At that time, far from having any influence on European affairs, the Hungarian Prime Minister was trying to contain the pressure from Brussels on his national policy.

---

[46] In France, the CSA's six advisors are appointed by the National Assembly and Senate (three each), and its chairman by the President of the Republic himself.

[47] In July 2019, faced with the possibility of his party's exclusion from the EPP, the Hungarian Prime Minister was reduced to detailing the Hungarian media landscape: "Today, there is a clear majority of media strongly critical of the government in Hungary. RTL Club is the biggest private TV channel; ATV is the biggest news channel; Népszava is the biggest daily; HVG is the biggest political weekly; Blikk is the biggest tabloid. As far as Internet portals are concerned, 80% of the Hungarian audience prefers the left-liberal, anti-government media platforms. To say nothing of the unlimited freedom of expression on social networks."

This pressure is growing. Shortly after Hungary's new constitution came into force, on January 18, 2012, Orbán appeared in the European Parliament for his first debate. In the eyes of many Hungarians, the Prime Minister played the role of a resistance fighter in the face of a new empire. He is the advocate of the nation against the foreigner, a role well served by the anger of certain MEPs. Daniel Cohn-Bendit, for example, did not realize that he is rallying Hungary behind its Prime Minister by entertaining the Chamber with his sarcasm. A few days later, the second round of the tug-of-war with the European institutions took place at home: Fidesz organized a "peace march" in which over 100,000 Hungarians took part in support of their government.

The EU's Achilles heel lies in its out-of-touch dimension and democratic deficit. The Hungarian Prime Minister is making sure that this weakness is exploited with all the popular fervor he enjoys.

Brussels's recriminations against Hungary's reforms led to the adoption of the Tavares report on July 3, 2013. The day before, Viktor Orbán had again gone to the European Parliament to defend the direction the country had been taking for three years with undeniable success. The Hungarian government conceded a few concessions, and the Tavares report, although adopted, remained unimplemented. Orbán's asymmetrical struggle with the European institutions can be summed up as "two steps forward, half a step back," a strategy strangely reminiscent of that of the Hungarian Orders against the Viennese Court in the seventeenth century.

*

Under pressure from Brussels' institutional politics, Orbán has been multiplying his neighborly relations as well as his global prospects. "Little Hungary" is part of several overlapping or superimposed areas. First, the Carpathian Basin,[48] where 2.4 million Magyars still live outside the

---

[48] "The most important thing, given where we are, is our project to rebuild the entire Carpathian Basin. I believe we are at an historic moment, marked by the end of Hungary's hundred-year solitude ... At last, let's really connect our countries! Let's connect our major cities with high-speed freeways and railroads ... We also propose to link our energy networks ... So we have a proposal for our neighbors: let's build the Carpathian Basin together. To achieve this, an attitude of mutual respect is of course essential, and our proposal can only stand in this spirit. Mutual respect in turn calls for plain speaking." Viktor Orbán, Tusványos speech, 2018.

borders inherited from the Treaty of Trianon: Hungarian influence extends here without irredentism, inviting neighboring states to develop in a positive way. Next comes the Visegrád group, which guarantees the defense of common interests within the EU. Beyond the V4 and the Carpathian Mountains, Hungary lies at the heart of a much larger geographical area: the "three seas" (Baltic, Adriatic and Black). This region, devoid of internal coherence, forms the limits of three former imperial powers: Germany, Russia, and Turkey. Part of the West and part of Eurasia, it is also a region with obvious economic potential and a population of 150 million with global resonances – far from China, but on the Silk Road nevertheless, and Orbán's recent contacts with China have been far from insubstantial. Hungary is also far from the United States, but under the umbrella of American-led NATO military power that safeguards Europe, and with warm ties to the American right, including its virtually undisputed leader Donald Trump. Hungary can be defined as the pivot of this heterogeneous space. The paradigm shift from inconsistent periphery to pole of very high geopolitical value required a medium: Viktor Orbán.

What's left of nationalism?

Hungary's national revival has given the domestic and international opposition the opportunity to denounce a nationalist drift. But the opposite is true, all the more so for, torn apart by decades of witch-hunting and reduced to the status of a scarecrow, nationalism is probably not to be found where it is denounced.

Nationalism does not consist of people power mixed with love of country, or it would not have had such a deep effect on history. Such a definition is more suited to original socialism, whose main figures[49] were fundamentally anti-modern.

As we understand it, nationalism is not a constant in European history, but a novelty that emerged with the French Revolution, as the *ancien régime* collapsed and was overtaken by a new mobilizing ideology. Nationalism responds to liberalism. It provides the glue necessary for the

---

[49] Such as Pierre Leroux and Joseph Proud'hon. Popular sovereignty is effective insofar as it is direct, and therefore exercised on a small scale; community management at the local level.

continuation of collective life, at a time when liberalism is destroying the order that enshrined the nation by establishing a "social contract." It is a patriotism deformed by the needs of modernity. It incorporates a contractual and progressive dimension. It also cultivates the paradox of being both amnesiac and hypermnesic.[50] It is a return of idea against fact, of original sentiment against history, and of passions against institutions – instead of tempering and enriching one with the other. Patriotism, on the other hand, is territorialized, identified with stable references and rooted in the long term. A difference of nature, not of degree, separates the two notions. To regard one as an excessive form of the other is to delegitimize the fatherland, which is seen as the seed of a dangerous obsession. In this respect, the national sentiment cultivated in Hungary since 2010 excludes nationalism.

*

There is no question here of putting nationalism on trial. Rather, it is a question of grasping it in its present-day character and at the end of a proven evolution. Indeed, as nationalism has accompanied the liberal movement, it is no stranger to our times. The French Revolution set itself an extraordinary ambition: to transform a country of 25 million subjects, built up over thirteen centuries of monarchy, into a republic of equal citizens. It thus threw out the communal baby with the feudal bathwater.[51] The social contract proclaiming the sovereignty of the people was instituted without consulting them. This has determined the entire political trajectory of the contemporary era and explains why the age of "the people" was only the age of the masses.

Nationalism also corresponded to a wave of enthusiasm. In its deployment, it is less an ideology than the political expression of a vigor that intoxicates the whole of Europe. It was the result of a flourishing of European societies, particularly France. Imbalance and vitality are two complementary aspects of the national movement. It found both discipline

---

[50] It does not refer to any concrete experience. In France, for example, the myth of the Gauls versus the Franks was perpetuated during the Revolution by the ThirdEstate and the nobility.

[51] The expression comes from Jean-Claude Michéa, *Les mystères de la gauche*, Climat, 2013.

and apotheosis in the advent of Napoleon Bonaparte, the heroic face of the new era. Nationalism was the youth of Europe. In Italy and Germany in particular, liberals celebrated the springtime of their peoples through their ideals. It was Carbonarism, Mazzini's *Giovine Italia*, the epic of Garibaldi's Red Shirts, the student brotherhoods in Germany, and so on. We can speak of a dawn of modern nations, but the revolutionary baptism has heavily influenced their destinies.

Nationalism takes different forms in different countries. Beyond exalted national sentiment, it was always driven by the imperative need to reunite the body politic following the dismantling of the revolution. In Germany, the dissolution of the Holy Roman Empire of *the German Nation* left Germans in an unprecedented and leaderless political vacuum. A keen observer of the early nineteenth century was not mistaken when he wrote:

"Those whom the dissolution of the German Empire and the act of confederation of the Rhine have lowered from the rank of dynasts to the condition of subjects who impatiently put up with having for masters those whose equals they were, or believed themselves to be, aspire to overthrow an order of things of which their pride is indignant, and to replace all the governments of this country by a single one. With them conspire the men of the universities, and the youth imbued with their theories, and those who attribute to the division of Germany into small states the calamities poured upon it by so many wars of which it is the continual theater. The unity of the German fatherland is their cry, their dogma, their religion exalted to the point of fanaticism, and this fanaticism has even won over the princes currently reigning. This unity, which France could have had nothing to fear when it possessed the left bank of the Rhine and Belgium, would now be of the utmost consequence to it. Who, moreover, can foresee the consequences of shaking a mass such as Germany, when its divided elements become agitated and confused? Who knows where the impulse would stop once it had been given?"[52]

This idealistic fever makes light of the historical heritage – imperfect, no doubt – in which a collective consciousness of the countries of Europe had been built up, a consciousness of identity long perpetuated by the Habsburgs in Central Europe.

It is a common misconception that there is a gulf between nationalism in France and nationalism in Germany. Revolutionary France was responsible for the rebuilding of German unity in three ways: through the historical frameworks it had dismantled, through the feelings of revenge inspired by the triumph of its arms, and through the new ideas it spread with its conquests. The Germanic world, once unified in the Holy Roman Empire, is returning to a unitary destiny through the modern nation first experimented in France. Johann Gottlieb Fichte's *Discourses to the German Nation*[53] have been proclaiming this since 1807: Germany exists beyond all its component parts. Geographical continuity made it easy to unify the various entities, as Prussia did under Chancellor Otto von Bismarck in 1864-1871. Nations rise up and isolate themselves, abandoning old legitimacies. Nationalism was thus inseparable from the liberal emancipatory tropism. Bismarck, the architect of a national Europe, wanted to detach the Czechs from Austria during the war of 1866. The King of Prussia issued a proclamation to the "Glorious Kingdom," extolling its historic rights and privileges. Napoleon had done the same for the Hungarians and Poles, as did Napoleon III for the Italians. This interplay of "liberty" and "tyranny" reproduced the plot of Mozart's *Magic Flute*: the wise and virtuous "Sarastro" of liberalism triumphs over the vindictive and murderous "Queen of the Night" of Reaction.

Three significant aspects of nationalism in Europe should therefore be borne in mind: 1) it was born with revolutionary ideology; 2) its contagious nature was part of the expansion of modernity; and 3) its adaptation in different countries led to a separation between peoples

---

[52] Congress of Vienna - Correspondence from Talleyrand to Louis XVIII, sixth letter, October 17, 1814, in *Mémoires*, C. M. de Talleyrand, Robert Laffont, Bouquins collection, 2007.
[53] These lectures, given at the University of Berlin, were fundamental to the fight for German unity.

formerly united in the bosom of Christendom.

Identity can be defined as man's *concrete* relationships with his own people, his past and his territory. Turning identity into an ideology seems contradictory from the outset. Yet this is how a deleterious trend in nationalism can be explained. An exclusive, self-centered, unitary aspiration leads to the rejection of all otherness. Nationalism feeds a first totalitarian tendency, born of revolutionary unanimity, which can be called "the ideology of the self." Nationalism thus pays the price for its original contradiction: to bring together a people, essentially a community of families forged over time, in a contractual and ideological process.

The rejection of all otherness is matched by the denial of all otherness, the ideology of sameness.[54] Self-affirmation and denial of the other both stem from revolutionary unanimity and form the twin matrices of totalitarianism. A denial of the other that is now supported by the liberal West.

*

Viktor Orbán heads the Hungarian government and presides over Fidesz, which enjoys a constitutional majority in Parliament. He does not just dispatch current affairs, he governs. This concentration and visibility of power contrasts with liberal logic, which undermines the verticality of power while at the same time erasing popular sovereignty. Popular sovereignty disappears without a visible successor. The head melts into the body. This confusion gives rise to a faceless counter-elite best characterized by its economic preponderance. Influence everywhere, authority nowhere. The perilous grandeur of a leader is replaced by the obscure power of networks, agents, and corporations. Their effective power flourishes in the shadow of the people's official but thoroughly undermined legitimacy. They are crowned in order to alienate them: their proclaimed sovereignty is the artifice needed to domesticate them.

This development is no accident, since liberalism, which recognizes only individuals, claims to emancipate the people from their communal dimension. In other words, the perennial and irreducible dimension to which the peoples of Central Europe were confined in their reverses of

---

[54] Alain de Benoist, *Les démons du bien*, Éditions Pierre-Guillaume de Roux, 2013.

fortune. For it was only the "legal country" that was shattered; the people of memory, mores, and culture endures under the denial of an elite that is effectively off the ground or sold out to the masters of the day. When the people fall off the radar of public power, and institutions exist at their own expense only to muzzle them, it is up to the people to recognize and identify themselves. If they succeed, then the death knell will sound for representatives who represent only themselves, conservatives who preserve only themselves, and political families reduced to mere coteries.

Central Europe's resources in the current situation

The liberal fog is lifting over continuities that have been shaken, but not broken. Central Europe is admirably equipped for the present, because its history has prepared it in a privileged way to overcome a modernity that is foreign and harmful to it. You can only destroy what you replace, and this region, both unitary and national, has never known an alternative model: neither a favorable order within which to forget its past, nor antagonistic national trajectories making its peoples irreconcilable. There is no doubt or dogma that calls into question this concert of small nations which, symbolically, have identified and come together over the centuries in Visegrád. The time has come for the whole of Europe to listen to the salutary murmur of our times, which Milan Kundera already sensed when the Iron Curtain was shaking: "This is why, in this region of small nations that have not yet perished, the vulnerability of Europe, of the whole of Europe, was visible more clearly and earlier than elsewhere ... In this sense, the destiny of Central Europe appears as an anticipation of European destiny in general, and its culture immediately takes on an enormous topicality."[55]

*

The Visegrád countries have tamed ethnonational modernity to their liking. For them, nationalism has not delegitimized the nation, but has for a time modified its political expression. It has simply imposed itself as the framework for a collective existence that has been perpetuated for centuries. While the nation-state in Central Europe corresponds to the

---

[55] Milan Kundera, op. cit.

Western model, the country's profound identity is not limited to it. We can distinguish two opposing types of state: *patrimonial* or *colonial* – and infinite trends in between. Today's Hungary and Poland clearly belong to the first type. The second exists without a nation, or separately from it. It is instituted by foreign indulgences, established on disembodied aspirations and thus alien to the people of which it is the legal emanation. This kind of state is colonial, in the sense that it establishes itself as the metropolis of an exploited country, or even as the relay of the hegemonic power of the moment. This misuse of public power is a major trend in recent history. Even the nation-state runs the risk of becoming a state without a nation, as illustrated by Jérôme Fourquet's recent essay, *L'archipel français*.[56]

Not only are the peoples of Central Europe endowed with heritage states, but their shared history has given them a penchant for concerted action and the complementary use of their strengths. For this reason alone, the Europe they prefigure has greater political consistency than the Union that has been attempted in Brussels for decades. The West is exhausting itself trying to compensate through law for the emptiness caused by the loss of meaning and the general disaffiliation of men and societies. Central Europe maintains itself by remembering who it is, both through its origins and through the civilizational heritage of Greece, Rome and Christianity. The Visegrád countries know the passion of freedom and the price of the sacrifices it demands, but also the illusions on which it feeds. They know that continuities conceal more freedoms than ruptures: you could not be less liberal.

The demanding path of civilization is to cultivate together the people and the order in which they are rooted in history. Let us beware of pitting "what unites us" against "what separates us," for those concepts are mutually nourishing: they are not enemy principles, but mutually fruitful forces. Nothing irreconcilable divides us, and nothing unique standardizes us. The mirage of being exclusive undermines the healthy ambition to be distinct: wanting to be everything is the surest way to be nothing. From this perspective, European patriotism is defined as the reverberation of national patriotisms on the challenges of the century.

---

[56] Jérôme Fourquet, *L'Archipel français*, Le Seuil, 2019.

VI.

The new battlefield

Viktor Orbán has been playing openly to win since his return to Hungary's premiership. His affirmation of a civic Hungary was accompanied by a theoretical content: *illiberal democracy* as opposed to *liberal democracy*. An ideological divide now runs through Europe's conservative camp, which separated Orbán from and the presidents of the European Commission, Jean-Claude Juncker (2014-2019) and Ursula von der Leyen (2019-). Ideological positions concealed unpredictable political options in the "pre-war" year of 2014, however. The fact remains that neither side can be reduced to its ideology: it conceals other logics in the closed field of economic warfare, itself a matrix of multiple conflicts.

A raw antagonism

> *"It is a victory whose full impact is yet to be measured."*
> Viktor Orbán on the evening of his re-election, April 6, 2014

Hungary faced a key election year in 2014. Viktor Orbán, who was again up for reelection with the shadow of his 2002 defeat still lurking, knew he was in for a big challenge after four years of government against the tide. The parliamentary elections took place on April 6 and Hungary's European elections on May 25. The first round confirmed the success of the 2010 Fidesz revolution, with the renewal of its two-thirds majority in the Hungarian Parliament. The next priority was international. After being sworn in, the reappointed Prime Minister declared "I consider extremist and dangerous for the Hungarian people a policy that proposes to sacrifice Hungary's thousand-year-old history on the altar of a kind of United States of Europe." In the May elections, the Conservative bloc's legitimacy was confirmed when it won 51.5% of the vote against a dispersed opposition.

On July 26, 2014, Orbán devoted his Tusványos speech on the illiberal democratic model that he wanted to develop in Hungary, a model that could set an example.

*

History shined a brighter light on the present as Hungary made its comeback. It was no longer a question of existing in the eyes of the West or in the shadow of its hegemony. Rather, it was a question of opposing its drifts with a specificity that is rich in future. This clarification has been painful. Firstly, because the international environment was plunging Europe, in spite of itself, into *decisive years*, as Spengler described them.[57] Secondly, because the suicidal tendencies of part of the continent forced the salutary tendencies to assert themselves ruthlessly. A century after the outbreak of the Great War, the conflict in the Ukraine, the rise of the Islamic State, and the migrations resulting from the conflagration in the Middle East set the scene for the emerging century – a singularly twilight dawn. Europe collapses while its neighbors implode.

A brief review of the European unrest of 2014 reveals the unravelling of the continent's liberal software as Hungary acquired a surprising political density, so much so that Viktor Orbán became the herald of Central Europe, if not global conservatism. The curves cross. The Carolingian metropolis sank into feverishness, while the Visegrád periphery learned to coordinate and gained self-confidence. The fragility of this evolution lay in its novelty. The retaliatory measures taken by Brussels (or to be more precise, by the interests that dominate there) are also part of the return of history. Like the internal conflicts in Hungary in the late 2000s, where there had been a will, there was a way. And where there was discipline, there was a school. Coercive liberalism adorned with cosmopolitan obsession provided Central Europe with a school of resistance to overcome its own lethargy and soon, with the strength accumulated in resistance, to deploy an ambition worthy of it.

*

At the opposite end of the spectrum from the liberal mantra *"laissez*

---

[57] Oswald Splengler, *The Decisive Years*, 1933.

faire, laissez passer," illiberalism is understood as "taking back control." Its orientation is not dogmatic, but at least it is based on popular demands for respect and security. Viktor Orbán's opponents at home and abroad condemn him as a traitor to the West. The criticism is accurate in one sense, since the tailor-made Magyar model evades certain globalist standards. It pits political power, endowed with popular legitimacy, against the unsurpassable authority of axiologically neutral law. At this point, the conflict between democracy and liberalism takes an explicit turn. For one, the people's vote; for the other, the rule of law.

The rule of law in question

Viktor Orbán was opposed to the nomination of Jean-Claude Juncker in 2014, despite his heading the EPP's list to head the European Commission. Only David Cameron shared Orbán's declared hostility to the Luxembourger, on the grounds that the latter defended a federalist agenda unacceptable to the United Kingdom, which would just two years later vote to leave the EU. On June 27, 2014, the European Council voted unanimously to appoint Jean-Claude Juncker, minus the Hungarian and British votes. In retaliation, Tibor Navracsics, the Hungarian candidate for the post of Commissioner, was subjected to a series of hardships in order to obtain the Education, Culture, Youth, and Citizenship portfolio. After an inquisitorial hearing before the European Parliament, MEPs found him so suspicious that they stripped him of the citizenship portfolio, replacing it with Sport.

The Juncker Commission took office on November 1, 2014, while Matteo Renzi's Italy held the rotating presidency of the European Union. On November 14, the Commission issued a document[58] proposing better guarantees for "rule of law" in the European Union. But the EU's strategic program, adopted by the European Council to set priorities for the 2014-2019 legislative period, include no action to be taken in this area. On December 16, EU foreign ministers agreed to hold an annual dialogue on "respect for the rule of law." The objective was to establish degrees up to the activation of Article 7 of the TFEU, by which a member state can be

---

[58] cf. Communication 15206/14 "Guaranteeing respect for the rule of law in the European Union."

expelled from the Union.

The liberal order appeared to be serenely successful; it anticipated or remedied any alarming eventuality. The coercive framework taking shape intentionally established deterrence: in the hushed world of Brussels, Article 7 is regarded as a "legal nuclear bomb." Poland[59] was the first country to be confronted with it, in relation to the reform of its judicial system. Then came Hungary's turn[60] for its alleged breaches of the rule of law. Initiated in one case by the Commission and in the other by the EU Parliament, the procedure remains incomplete, and not without reason. What would be the real scope and applicability of "political excommunication?" Wouldn't such a humiliation inflicted on a member state be the worst blow to the European cohesion the EU claims to defend?

The crucial importance of the rule of law in the EU was demonstrated by the portfolio of Frans Timmermans, First Vice-President "responsible for better lawmaking, inter-institutional relations, the rule of law and the Charter of Fundamental Rights." A Dutchman and leader of the Socialists in the 2014 European elections, Timmermans became the *bête noire* of the illiberal democracies asserting themselves in the years 2014-2019.

*

What is the rule of law? An institutional system in which public power is subject to the law. Hungary subscribes to this framework, without which the international animosity since 2010 would not have been confined to "suspicions," and the Venice Commission[61] would not have amicably resolved its differences with Budapest. Hungary's political elites, however, also intend to contain subversive applications of a law that is abusively neutral. They adopt a practical rather than a dogmatic approach. They refuse to allow a particular interest to take precedence over the general interest, since the public authorities are the guarantors of the latter.

---

[59] Activation triggered on December 20, 2017, by the European Commission. The procedure requires not only the Commission's endorsement, but also a two-thirds majority vote in Parliament and a qualified majority in the EU Council.

[60] Activation triggered on September 12, 2018, following Parliament's adoption of the Sargentini report.

[61] The Venice Commission is a consultative body of the Council of Europe "for democracy through law."

The intention is to ensure that legal control does not turn into political mutilation. According to illiberal thinking, law does not base its authority in itself, but in a political body that institutes it. Subsidiarily, it rests on the sovereignty of the same body politic, now embodied in the electorate and consulted by the vote. The rule of law contributes to the common good, but it is not enough; the spirit must prevail over the letter.

At the opposite end of the spectrum are the dogmatic advocates of the rule of law, who favor disembodied international sovereignty over democratic sovereignty. The public authorities of each nation would be obliged, on the one hand, to obey an international law of indeterminate contours, and on the other, to protect the individual, defined by his or her choices alone. The fatal complementarity of international institutions and minority demands illustrates this subversion.[62] That public power is dedicated to such services is expressed in a National Assembly report[63] dated October 2018. It assigns to rule of law the purpose that "the distribution of powers aims to open up the widest possible space for individual freedoms." This is a far cry from the simple, probing application of the law.

Presented as egalitarian progress, the rule of law conceals other relations of power, and runs the risk of being debased to the benefit of a few: translucent in its neutrality, it quickly becomes opaque in practice. An invincible influence steers the interpretation of the law to the benefit of *certain* particular interests.[64] This exposes the most vulnerable to the mercy of the most ambitious, the richest and the most mobile; in the words of Napoleon, both jurist and soldier: "the habit of the most violent facts wears less on the heart than abstractions; soldiers are better than lawyers."

Excess is compounded by contradiction. The sovereignty of

---

[62] The "Global Compact on Migration" or Marrakech Pact was adopted on December 19, 2018, by the United Nations General Assembly. It lays the groundwork for an international responsibility to which states will be subject under the rule of law. Every individual is given a "right to migrate."

[63] Report 1299 entitled: "Respect for the rule of law in the European Union"

[64] Judith Varga, Hungary's Minister of Justice, lamented this in her speech to MEPs on April 14, 2020: "The fundamental values of the EU, including the rule of law, are our common values, and for us flow from the source. Can an institution proclaim itself the guardian of the rule of law if it turns the rule of law into a political tool, an instrument of exclusion and division?"

axiologically neutral law rests on a paradox: common obedience to every man for himself. A strange unitary aspiration around a dissolving principle: this is the final word of liberal communion - and its final word.

The rule of law covers, like ivy, conflicts driven by the eternal thirst for power. In liberal Europe, ideological correctness pays for its subordination to economic interests: they are the only authorized superego of our time. The energy question, explosive in 2014 in the context of the Ukrainian crisis, illustrates this eloquently.

Revealing the great energy game

Between 2007 and 2012, the European Union negotiated an ambitious association agreement with Ukraine, committing the country to Western integration. As the signing of the agreement loomed in November 2013, the pro-Russian Ukrainian government turned its back on the EU, with the intention of maintaining a pivotal role between the Russian world and the West.

This turnabout exasperated part of the Ukrainian population and irritated the United States. Demonstrations in Kiev soon became the scene of spectacular clashes with government forces; they culminated in February 2014 in the Maidan revolution, which overthrew the government of Viktor Yanukovych. Unrest broke out in the east of the country, and the Donbas regions, led by pro-Moscow separatists soon seceded and Russia annexed Crimea. The battle for Ukraine leads to war in Ukraine. The escalation of a new conflict looms over the continent.

The main victim was Ukraine – prey to be snatched up from east to west with no consideration for the misery of the people, not even in the eyes of their corrupt elites or the international community. The EU intended to link Ukraine's market to its own,[65] not out of charity, but for the benefit of its companies. Instead it found itself shackled to a distressed country that became even more perilous after the renewed Russian invasion of February 2022. Only accession to the status of member state could place Kiev in a position to benefit from the EU, and this prospect is scarcely conceivable. Emigration is bleeding Ukraine dry, who receive the refugees for ideological reasons and as a new source of inexpensive labor.

---

[65] The agreement was finally signed shortly after the coup, on March 21, 2014.

The situation has also poisoned relations between the EU and Russia for a long time to come.

*

Brussels's real power lies in its role as an arbiter with regard to the subordination of member states to the internal European market. The interdependence of nations naturally increases EU prerogatives: any dysfunction then demands a European response inspired by the interests best defended in Brussels. With the Ukrainian crisis, European dysfunction is facing the return of history. Liberal criticism of politics is not enough to lead. The Ukrainian crisis has revealed the EU's strategic weakness, the decisive influence of American will through NATO and unilateral diplomacy, and the real balance of power within the Union.

Despite Brussels's pusillanimity and American hegemony, *realpolitik* continues to dictate. Russia remains an essential partner in the EU's energy supply despite the war. As Germany and Russia continue their energy rapprochement, who in the EU is paying for the collateral damage of the Ukrainian crisis? Those who do not have the strength to defend their interests. The countries of southeastern Europe are largely dependent on Russian gas and have been defending gas supplies via the Black Sea. The Ukrainian crisis provided an excellent pretext for scuttling South Stream, which was cancelled in December 2014. The renewed war of 2022 also resulted in the effective sabotage, apparently by Ukrainian special forces, of the Nord Stream 1 and 2 Pipelines in September of that year. Orbán, however, has maintained a more practical position, continuing to engage Russia in energy purchases, offering the practical explanation that Hungary simply needs Russian gas to survive. Hungary's audacity nevertheless infuriated the United States and the EU elites in Brussels: the influential American Senator John McCain called the Hungarian Prime Minister a "neo-fascist dictator" in part for his friendlier attitude toward Russia.

While American pressure presented a clear obstacle to South Stream, the EU created a paradox. Strangely enough, the Nord Stream project, South Stream's twin and direct supplier to Germany via the Baltic Sea, did not come under the same attack from the European Commission, or anything other than rhetorical opposition before its sabotage in 2022, after which Germany launched a criminal investigation and in August 2024 indicted one of the alleged Ukrainian perpetrators. It would seem that the obligation to break with Russia over disfavored foreign policy varies according to the vulnerability of European countries and their clout in Brussels.

*

Until now, the countries of Central Europe have never been able to stop the decisions of the EU's major players. They balk, but eat their hats, and, as we shall see with regard to the migration crisis, are sometimes punished anyway.

VII.

The tipping point of the migration crisis

The Visegrád countries have formed a pole of resistance, taking advantage of a major fault of the liberal system: having allowed and defended the migratory tsunami of 2015. That event has left an indelible mark on the collective memory of the peoples of Central Europe, subjecting their leaders to a baptism of fire. It is the crucible of an alternative and audible political line and the challenge, through its Achilles' heel, of an ideology that has been hegemonic for decades.

Crash and tsunami in the Mediterranean

On June 29, 2014, two days before the new European Parliament took office, Abu Bakr Al-Baghdadi proclaimed a new Caliphate in the Mosul mosque in the name of the Islamic State. The dazzling success of ISIS's radical jihadists illustrated the state of decay in Iraq since the American invasion in 2003 and Syria's weakness since its unrest began in 2011. That year's Arab Spring also destabilized the southern shores of the Mediterranean. Libya collapsed into anarchy with the fall of Muammar Gaddafi. Algeria is in a state of crisis. Egypt passed through crisis and turned into a military dictatorship far more oppressive than the previous one. In Sub-Saharan Africa, seven national governments were overthrown by coups between 2020 and 2023, while Islamist organizations gain traction across the North and West of the continent. Long gone are the days when the Ottoman Empire was known as the Sick Man of Europe, when the whole world accepted the preeminence of the powers of the old continent. For Iran and Turkey alike, the sun rose in the West. The constitutional revolution in Teheran (1905-1911) and that of the Young Turks (1908) on the shores of the Bosphorus bore witness to the irresistible ascendancy of European models before the great conflagration of 1914.

Decolonization reversed this trend. In the 1950s, Colonel Nasser nationalized the Suez Canal and Europe lost control of its energy supplies in the region. Arab nationalism marked the point of balance in this game of influence between the Muslim East and Europe. The Islamic revolution in Iran led to the sanctuarization of national resources, but also to secession from the Western model of society. Islam returned to the heart of public life.

The first failure of the EU, and of the West generally, was to allow the destabilization of the east and even exacerbate it. The Arab Spring was celebrated as an affirmation of the modernity of these countries. The extreme left in France called for their spread north of the Mediterranean, while the former American Vice President and failed Democratic 2000 presidential candidate Al Gore called for "an American Spring." American-led NATO action led directly to Libya's destabilization.

Only the Syrian state, ruled with an iron fist by Bashar El-Assad, held its own in the turmoil. The Syrian civil war, or international war in Syria, owes its ruthlessness to the strategic as well as religious stakes underlying it. Here again, it was a question of energy and strategic assets. The overland transport of hydrocarbons from the Persian Gulf to the Mediterranean coast necessarily passes through Syria. The Syrian government's preference for the Iranian pipeline project, to the detriment of Qatar, preceded the start of the insurrection by a few weeks. Russia also looked covetously at Syria in its hour of need for future military bases.

While the East escapes Western determinisms inherited from the last century, Europe pursues the mirage of a universal consensus around its demonetized slogans; it responds to the return of history with a more complete denial. The number of refugees worldwide rose from 19.4 million in 2005 to 53 million in 2015[66] to 281 million in 2024. Migration thus poses a global political problem, behind the moralizing smokescreen. From a certain point of view, it is even a highly immoral issue: the International Organization for Migration (IOM) estimated the turnover of illegal immigrant trafficking at between 3 and 10 billion euros a year by 2015 alone.[67] Following the expansion of the Islamic State, the influx of

---

[66] cf. Jean-Baptiste Noé, *La crise migratoire*, Bernard Giovanangeli Éditeur, 2015.
[67] Jean-Baptiste Noé, ibid.

migrants via Turkey and the Balkans grew exponentially.[68] Europe failed to react decisively to remedy the situation. The cataclysmic aspect of the migratory wave struck Europeans on April 19, 2015, when the sinking of a migrant boat off the island of Lampedusa led to the drowning of 400 passengers. Yet the Italian navy continued to rescue boats adrift in its territorial waters: 10,000 people were rescued over the weekend of April 11 and 12 alone.[69] Throughout the spring and summer of 2015, the tidal wave flooded Europe via Libya and above all the Balkans with over 100,000 entries in July alone. On August 19, 2015, German Chancellor Angela Merkel set her country's reception capacity at 800,000 refugees, which amounts to imposing them on the other members of the Schengen area.

*

This headlong rush was vindicated by the Aylan affair. On the night of September 2-3, 2015, a makeshift boat loaded with migrants sank between the Turkish coast and the island of Kos. Twelve of the 32 passengers died. Among the victims was a three year-old child named Aylan Kurdi, whose corpse was found washed up on a Turkish beach the following day and complacently photographed. A deafening press campaign was unleashed across the continent, as if every European shared guilt for his death, and that the way to atone for this fault was to welcome the migratory wave unconditionally.[70] Responsibility for this lies first and foremost with Angela Merkel, who declared on August 31: "Wir schaffen das!" (We can do it). The European consensus seemed to be aligned with Berlin's emotional power grab. On September 3, French President François Hollande tweeted his joint intention with Angela Merkel to set

---

[68] 60,000 people in 2013, 219,000 in 2014. Frontex figures.

[69] Jean-Baptiste Noé, ibid.

[70] A reminder of the facts. Born in Kobane, near the Turkish border, the Kurds find themselves in the heart of an intense combat zone, which explains their flight north. After unsuccessful attempts to obtain a Canadian visa, the father decided to flee with his family to the island of Kos, a Greek territory only four kilometers from the Turkish coast: an attempt to leave a safe zone to enter the European Union and the Schengen area illegally, provoked by the ripple effect and the perception of the welcoming discourse of European leaders. It was only on March 13, 2020, that the Turkish courts handed down their verdict, sentencing three smugglers to 125 years in prison.

up "a permanent and compulsory reception mechanism for refugees."

Mention of migrant quotas had appeared in European texts as early as Spring 2015. On May 27, the Commission reported on the evolution of its migration agenda. It included a proposal for "resettlement" on a voluntary basis.[71] Viktor Orbán immediately denounced this as a "crazy plan." On June 26, a European summit was held in Brussels. The "temporary and exceptional relocation over two years ... of 40,000 people" was adopted by qualified majority, despite opposition from Hungary, Slovakia, and the Czech Republic. The United Kingdom, more sparingly disposed and ready to begin accepting hundreds of thousands of migrants a year despite a Conservative government nominally opposed to illegal migration, opted out of the quotas from the outset.

Taking advantage of the shockwaves generated by the Aylan affair, on September 9 the Commission proposed another plan for the distribution of 120,000 new migrants, three times the figure announced at the beginning of the summer. The choice of a certain number of relocations, between zero and all asylum seekers, seems arbitrary. But since it is part of a plan, observers expect to follow its application to understand its logic; but there is none. Media hysteria has simply unleashed the Brussels bureaucracy.

The "distribution keys" sow the seeds of unease, as they select the quantities of migrants to be distributed as well as the host countries, which are requisitioned like barracks. That the mainspring of this dismal accounting is to be found in maudlin humanitarianism and the nauseating exploitation of a child's drowning only served to open our eyes to the extent to which liberal elites had gone astray. Migrant quotas are a precious testimony to liberalism at the end of its life: they signal the start of palliative care and provoke a reaction from countries that do not want to die.

The Aylan affair was undoubtedly the historic turning point at which the liberal elites' relationship with migration tipped definitively into the absurd. At that moment, the countries of the Visegrád group had the choice

---

[71] "The Commission has adopted a recommendation inviting Member States to resettle, over a two-year period, 20,000 people from third countries recognized by the UNHCR as being in clear need of international protection, according to a distribution key (see Annex 3). Member States participating in the program will be entitled to financial assistance, with the EU making €50 million available over the 2015-2016 period."

of resigning themselves or standing up: by following Viktor Orbán's lead, they rescued everything in Europe that escaped resignation. A distinction has been made between a living Europe and the liberal precipice, between peoples whose very existence is suddenly questioned and the obstinate militants of their negation. It was a revolution because it forced us to choose. From this moment onwards, all other events have worked to separate the two tendencies instead of bringing them closer together.

The rebirth of the Visegrád group

Hungary lies at the southeastern end of the Schengen area, opposite Serbia, Romania, and Croatia (the latter two countries being both in the EU and outside Schengen). This situation imposes strict obligations in terms of border control. Greece, absolutely overwhelmed and economically devastated, is not fulfilling its mission. After all, the illegal immigrants want to reach the wealthier northern countries. But the terrible summer forced the reluctant countries of Central Europe to take the lead. In June 2015, Hungary decided to build a barrier on the Serbian border. A barrage of criticism condemned the "barrier of shame," while the progress of the work still failed to stem illegal immigration. Central Europe stands united. On September 11, in Prague, the head of Czech diplomacy, Lubomir Zaoralek, declared that the countries of the Visegrád group refused to accept the migrant quotas that the European Union wanted to impose on them. Hungary followed suit, amending the Penal Code to make crossing the border a criminal offence. It then passed a law authorizing the government to deploy its army at the borders and to use non-lethal weapons, such as rubber bullets and tear gas grenades, against migrants.[72] This marked the start of a back-pedal at European level. On September 13, Merkel suspended the Schengen agreements: Germany closed its border with Austria and implicitly instructed the transit countries to stem the flow. The European summit on September 23 confirmed the EU's political division into two camps on the migration issue. For the first time, the countries of Central Europe formed a camp of their own, rather than serving as auxiliaries to the dominant nations.

After a noticeable lull during the winter, immigration rose again in

---

[72] Jean-Baptiste Noé, ibid.

2016. Following Hungary's example, Slovenia, also a guarantor of the Schengen area, announced on March 8 that it would close its border to all illegal immigrants, with humanitarian exceptions. Serbia and Croatia followed suit. Macedonia immediately announced that it would accept the same number of illegal immigrants as Serbia (so as not to keep any).

*

One of the major consequences of the migration crisis came in the autumn of 2015, with the holding of parliamentary elections in Poland. On October 25, both chambers of the Polish Parliament were renewed, with the conservative Law and Justice party (PiS) winning 37.58% of the vote to the Civic Platform's 24%. This result came as a surprise both in Poland and abroad, as the polls had placed the liberal right in an advantageous position. But Donald Tusk, its leading figure, has chaired the EU Council since 2014. His closeness to Angela Merkel was skillfully exploited by the opposition. The time had come for Jarosław Kaczyński's party to exact revenge, with an absolute majority in both the Sejm and the Senate, a success unseen since the post-communist transition. Poland and Hungary share many affinities, and the PiS and Fidesz are not without similarities. The electoral year 2015 in Poland was equivalent to 2010 in Hungary, though not, given the results of the 2024 election, not as long-lived. The PiS's first experience of power, between 2005 and 2007, was reminiscent of Viktor Orbán's first term of office, from 1998 to 2002. In Kaczyński, the Fidesz president found his emulator north of the Carpathians. The two party leaders met on January 6, 2016, in a town in southern Poland where they discussed a future of unity: and how to build "Budapest on the Vistula."

This political change in Poland was of great help to Viktor Orbán. Beyond migration policy, the two countries shared the same vision of Europe, based on conservative values. Each country covers the other, widening the field of action and hampering Brussels's ability to retaliate. In the wake of the migration issue, other illiberal topics could be put forward. For example, on March 31, 2016, Polish Prime Minister Beata Szydło announced on the radio that she was in favor of an integral pro-life policy. Poland's particular Catholic fervor explains this concern, but the announcement is part of the implementation of a natalist policy, as in Hungary. On April 14, the Polish parliament passed a law protecting Polish land from foreign investment, in favor of small farmers. Two weeks later,[73] a Polish government decree abolished the Anti-Discrimination Council, a body responsible for implementing an "open society."

These measures drew noisy disapproval from Brussels. But on Monday May 21, Poland rejected the European Commission's ultimatum to settle the dispute between the Polish state and the Constitutional Court. Warsaw dared to take a haughtier attitude than Budapest: a question of the country's critical size and political culture. But in both cases, the rejection of migration has served as a springboard for the formulation of a broader political alternative. A policy of generous redistribution towards the working classes and families has led to two complementary phenomena: the working classes identify with the conservative camp; the center and the left in opposition become supporters of liberal austerity.

As in Hungary in 2014, the verdict of the ballot box on October 13, 2019, for a time confirmed the political orientation assumed against all odds. The United Right, led by the PiS, won with 43.59%, renewing its absolute majority in the Sejm but narrowly missing out on the Senate. The election was also marked by the return to the Diet of a left-wing coalition (13%), embracing the principles of the open society in matters of gender theory and multiculturalism, which would go on to win back legislative power in 2024.

*

While there have been obvious similarities between Poland and Hungary, the Czech Republic has presented a very different political picture. It is true that Bohuslav Sobotka's[74] social-democratic government joined Viktor Orbán's fightback against the EU's migration policy. This option showed the extent to which the notion of social democracy does not cover the same reality in the center and west of the continent. But this old institutional party nonetheless felt the wrath of the populist wave in

---

[73] The Anti-Discrimination Council was set up on January 1, 2011.
[74] Founded in 1878, forcibly dissolved into the Communist Party in 1948 and reappearing in 1989, the ČSSD (Czech Social Democratic Party) is the historic political force of socialism in the Czech Republic.

October 2017, when elections brought billionaire Andrej Babiš and his ANO 2011 political party to power. Prague's new strongman, who held power until 2021 and remains popular, was dubbed the "Czech Trump," so distinguished is he by his immense wealth, business pragmatism, and a very direct style. He affected hostility toward immigration and opened Central European solidarity, in line with the aspirations of the electorate. Like the Poles, Babiš was content to follow the path paved by the Hungarians. Opposition to the dominant social democratic system was never his guiding principle, but the fact that he based his belated political career on this trend confirmed the winds of change.

Hungarian disinhibition and Western deprivation

Under Orbán, Hungary systematically explored room for legal maneuvering. Since the Lisbon Treaty came into force, member states have been entitled to ask the European Commission to reverse a decision if they can show that it legitimately falls to the national level.[75] This procedure requires the agreement of the parliaments of at least ten member states. To this end, on November 3, 2015, the Hungarian Parliament adopted called for the Commission to cancel the migrant distribution system proposed to the Council.

The legal aspect of the fight against migration was based on Hungary's 2011 constitution. On the fifth anniversary of its adoption,[76] Orbán declared: "To be perfectly clear and unequivocal, I can say that Islamization is constitutionally prohibited in Hungary." He contrasted this clarity with Western Europe, "in denial about its past and future, and burdened by self-flagellation." The Hungarian position is clear-cut, but not proselytizing. Fidesz's policy may attract emulators and opponents, but it only claims to embrace what it can. Hungary pleads first by example, then by search for an alternative consensus, both in terms of party membership and international diplomacy. This was the thrust of the Orbán's speech at the EPP summit held in Madrid on October 21-22, 2015. He repeated the exercise tirelessly, notably on the following April 15, at a meeting of the Centrist Democrat International (CDI) in Lisbon, contrasting the priority

---

[75] Under the principle of subsidiarity.
[76] April 25, 2016.

of border protection with asylum reform.

The strength of Hungary's anti-migration measures lies in democratic legitimacy. On May 3, 2016, the Hungarian Supreme Court authorized a referendum on the relocation of migrants. On October 2, 2016, 98% of the votes cast confirmed the political line taken by the government. The turnout was 41.32%, close to that of the 2002 referendum on membership of the European Union, but below the 50% quorum required.

*

In Bratislava, the SMER socialists[77] was leading a coalition government at the time. In 2015, with the support of Slovak public opinion, Prime Minister Robert Fico took the Council of the European Union to court, challenging the plan to distribute 160,000 refugees among EU member states. The case was referred to the Court of Justice in Luxembourg[78] under Article 263 of the Treaty on the Functioning of the European Union (TFEU), which allows each member state to appeal against any EU decision that infringes upon its rights. This offensive rhetoric against the quota policy satisfied the Slovak electorate. Despite the stress on his party, the outgoing Prime Minister came out on top in the parliamentary elections on March 5, 2016 and formed a new government coalition. Peripheral Europe defended its turf, enhanced by Slovakia's holding of the EU presidency in the second half of 2016. This passage into the limelight was not accompanied by any concrete progress, however. On May 25, Fico received Martin Schulz, President of the European Parliament in his capital as part of the imminent Slovak presidency. Fico asserted his rejection of both migrant quotas and a Muslim presence in Slovakia and denounced the manipulations of George Soros against the nations of Europe. This firm stance was softened as the representatives moved further away from the Carpathians. In Berlin, Slovakia's permanent representative to the European Union, Ivan Korčok, declared that Bratislava's main objective in taking over the EU presidency was to avoid fragmentation of the EU and to combat the

---

[77] A center-left party, SMER led government coalitions from 2006 to 2010 and since 2012.
[78] Action brought on December 2, 2015 (Case C-643/15). Hungary in turn lodged an appeal the following day (Case C-647/15).

perception of an East-West divide.

*

At the same time, the migration crisis is tearing the Liberals apart. On February 24, 2016, the Balkan states held a consultative meeting on the migration crisis in Vienna. The meeting was attended by representatives from Albania, Bulgaria, Kosovo, Croatia, Macedonia, Montenegro, Serbia, and Slovenia. Greece was not invited. Austrian Chancellor Werner Faymann declared that Athens was behaving "like a travel agency" by allowing migrants to pass freely through. Greece saw red and recalled its ambassador to Austria for consultations. Faymann's irritability can be explained by the growing hostility of public opinion to lax immigration policy. The verdict came down on May 9: Austria's SPÖ (Social Democratic Party of Austria) Chancellor resigned after eight years in office. He also stepped down as SPÖ chairman. This head of government had been very critical of resistance of Central European countries over the previous year, to the point of proposing economic sanctions against them.

The police authorities of Macedonia, Serbia, Croatia, and Slovenia meet representatives of Austria, the Dutch Presidency of the European Council, and Hungary in Belgrade. Athens was invited this time but refused to participate. The talks did little to help Macedonia, which was reduced to begging other member states for logistical support.

*

On April 19, 2016, Viktor Orbán was received by former German Chancellor Helmut Kohl. The architect of German reunification had at one time invited Fidesz to join the EPP. His vision of Christian democracy differed markedly from that of his successor Angela Merkel. Two days before receiving the Hungarian Prime Minister, Kohl declared in the *Tagesspiegel*: "The solution [to migration] lies in the regions affected. It is not in Europe. Europe cannot become a new home for millions of needy people around the world."[79] Merkel was not bothered by the muted opposition to migration running through Germany, but found herself at a loss when it came to international issues. Controlling immigration

---

[79] *Tagesspiegel*, April 17, 2016.

required, above all, an agreement with Recep Tayyip Erdoğan's Turkey.

On October 18, 2015, it was the German Chancellor alone who traveled to Istanbul to negotiate the containment of the refugee flood with the Turkish leader.[80] The emergency situation revealed a Germany that was hegemonic in Europe and inconsistent outside. Any unprecedented situation eluded the authority of law: relations were polarized by the balance of power, by the state of nature. Negotiation, designed to avoid conflict, led to capitulation. Worse still, Merkel had come to negotiate the curtailment of a flow she considers more of an inevitability than a calamity. So Turkey's demands have all the air of a tribute extorted from a beleaguered Byzantium. Erdoğan demanded a payment of three billion euros, the acceleration of EU accession negotiations for Turkish admission, and the liberalization of visas for Turkish citizens, in order to hold back the two million migrants still present in his country.

A climate of anxiety therefore prevailed during the negotiations for the agreement debated in the Council during the winter of 2016. On March 7, the European summit welcomed a distinguished guest, Turkey's Foreign Minister Ahmet Davutoğlu. The President of the European Council, Donald Tusk, declared that "the time for irregular immigration into Europe is over." In other words, migration must be organized, rather than stopped or reversed. In this sense, Merkel, Mark Rutte,[81] and Ahmet Davutoğlu attempted a *coup de main* by imposing on the Council an agreement drawn up without the knowledge of the other heads of state. This subversion failed in the face of an outcry from Central Europe, which postponed the adoption of a more consensual text until the March 18 summit.[82]

The compulsory visa regime for Turkish citizens was thus maintained, a fact welcomed by Peter Szijjarto on behalf of his Central European counterparts a few days later in Prague: "Only countries that meet all the

---

[80] Jean-Baptiste Noé, ibid.

[81] At the time, the Dutch Prime Minister held the rotating presidency of the European Union.

[82] The agreement includes the payment of 3 billion euros to Turkey. Above all, it ratifies an aberrant system of exchanging migrants between the EU and Turkey, on the basis of one migrant who entered the Union illegally being returned to Turkey for one Syrian migrant eligible for asylum in Europe. Asylum applications are now examined in Turkey, which has been declared a safe country.

criteria can obtain the visa-free regime. From our point of view, it would be unacceptable for Georgia and Ukraine to benefit after Turkey."[83]

The German Chancellor failed to conclude an EU-Turkey agreement ahead of regional elections. On March 13, the German federal states (*Länder*) of Sachsen-Anhalt, Baden-Württemberg, and Rheinpfalz held their parliamentary elections. The fledgling Alternative für Deutschland party[84] made historic gains, entering all three assemblies.[85] It was a thunderbolt for the CDU, which could not conceive of being challenged on the right, and for an entire country dominated by the ghosts of its past.

*

Islamic attacks played a role in the evolution of Western public opinion and in the formation of a trans-European civic concern about migration. As early as the attack on *Charlie Hebdo* on January 7, 2015, Viktor Orbán announced his position on mass migration. The attacks of November 13, on a completely different scale and in the wake of the migration crisis, justified their intransigence in the eyes of Central European governments and strengthened their public support. In April 2016, Brussels itself was hit by deadly attacks. It then appeared that, through their migration policies, Western states were primarily concerned with an idealized "other," to the detriment of the people from whom they derive their legitimacy and even their very existence.

For Hungary, the matter did not end there. After years of refusing to adhere to EU migration policies, in 2020 the Luxembourg court found Hungary in violation of them. In June 2024, a judge imposed a 200 million-euro fine to penalize Hungary, with an additional one million euros per each additional day of noncompliance. Orbán, whose party won the country's European elections that same month, shows no sign of paying.

These lessons allow us to approach the migration crisis with the

---

[83] Remarks made on May 4, 2016, at a meeting of Visegrad Group foreign ministers.
[84] Alternative für Deutschland (AfD) was launched in early 2013, against a backdrop of growing mistrust of the euro. The party appropriates identity-based themes at the pace of the migration crisis.
[85] 24.27% in Saxony-Anhalt, 15.10% in Baden-Wurtenberg and 12.61% in Rhineland-Palatinate.

necessary lucidity. First and foremost, Europe's economic weight makes it an unavoidable draw to the developing world. This attractiveness is a form of power. But the character of our age is to subordinate every other dimension of existence to it. Politics and war, to paraphrase Clausewitz, are merely the continuation of economics by other means. The obvious poverty of such conception exposes Europe to the risk of disappearing as a civilization while existing, if not exactly flourishing, as a market. After all, increased consumption depends on population growth. Asleep in relative prosperity, the Old World drifts under the prevailing international wind – a North American wind – as the United States posts the best post-Covid recovery figures of all industrial economies, while and China, once both admired and feared, recedes and the EU economies stagnate. Germany's economic zeal distracts it from all other considerations and make it part of the problem.

Greater clashes between Brussels and the Central European bloc seem inevitable and will indeed take place. The orchestra is playing, the officers are drunk, and it is up to ordinary sailors to take the helm. The countries of Central Europe are making history and can use their unique role to shape European and global politics.

VIII.

What's left of liberalism

The political response in Central Europe cannot be seen as ideological. The course of events is rather slow. There was no rush, but a response imprinted in history under the pressure of facts, a political work of circumstances, entirely dictated by the heavy and merciless necessity of not disappearing. This quiet dissent contrasts with the aberrant trajectory of liberal millenarianism.

The European superiority complex

The principle of resettlement is the fatal outcome of a number of joint trends: economic obsession, cosmopolitan obsession, increased migratory pressure, disregard for popular aspirations, misguided charity, and so on. Neither chance nor bad luck, but a tragic outcome. "The gods blind those they wish to lose." This sentence sheds light on the biased calculations of Jean-Claude Juncker, then a candidate for the presidency of the Commission, and the compulsory quotas they prefigure. His program[86] states: "Demographic projections show that by 2060, the EU's working population will have shrunk by more than 10%, or 50 million people, while the number of pensioners will increase by between 17.1% and 30%. This trend poses a real danger to the EU's economic productivity, particularly as soon there will be two members of the working population for every person over 65, instead of four as there are today."

We need to leave aside a biased analysis, which consists of extending curves over 45 years to justify a five-year program. Winston Churchill distinguished three forms of lying: by commission, by omission, and by statistics. The observation of a danger to the "economic productivity of the

---

[86] The EPP, program, entitled "Future," on April 23, 2014.

EU" is factual; long-term reflection would immediately prompt us to consider the essential point: that this decline indicates nihilism, a disgust with life, and that the public authorities must commit themselves to boosting the birth rate. But nothing happens. No attention is paid to the Europeans who are locking themselves into celibacy and sterility. No thought is given to the causes of this deleterious Malthusianism. No reflection on the millions of Europeans yet to be born, whom the bureaucrat crosses out with the same stroke of the pen as he dares to write "future" at the head of his program. This resignation illustrates the disloyalty of a caste and an era. It would be a great mistake to believe that this contempt is limited to Europeans. The Africans and Asians designated to take their place are not men coming to enlarge a family, but workers acquired for service: "We will need to fill the new jobs created to serve an ever-increasing number of elderly people, particularly in the care sector."[87]

To fit the unprecedented chapter in world history that is the demographic explosion of the South into the tiny epilogue of a Europe rotting with old age, and to subject the vitality of the former to the effacement of the latter: this is perhaps the most extraordinary testimony to Europe's sense of superiority and by far its most vain illusion. Having conquered peoples because it was more powerful, Europe expects them to come and serve it because it is rich and old. This is why, far from shedding the distressing illusions of the twentieth century, Europe continues to get lost in them.

*

What remains of this system, established to guarantee peace and freedom? The Juncker Commission began its mandate by refining the framework of the "rule of law," insensitively binding the countries brought together in the Union. Never before has Brussels had more extensive, yet softly contested, prerogatives. So much so, in fact, that in spring 2015, the REFIT reform[88] provided for less Community legislation, in a break with the Barroso Commission. Europe could then be seen as a tidy, unchanging

---

[87] Ibid.
[88] The REFIT program.

space, where the vagaries of history would be nothing more than adjustments and reasonable accommodations. A destiny under a bell jar, where the vagueness of grand principles would replace the peril of the open sea.

By concentrating a phenomenon that had already begun and is continuing, the migration crisis is giving history a new lease of life. The last decade has shown that life is far more generous than Juncker may have feared. Neither exhausted nor resigned, humanity springs up greener and newer with each generation. Life is generous, and cruel. Attacks, assaults: so many lives cut short as we await the worst that awaits Europeans thanks to the insensitivity to reality that characterizes liberal elites who are the least likely among Europeans to have to suffer it in their own cossetted lives.

Juncker and his emulators evoke the antipathy inspired by the Jacobins, under the Napoleonic Empire, in the young Alphonse de Lamartine: "All these geometric men, who alone had the world and who crushed us young men under the insolent tyranny of their triumph, believed they had dried up forever in us what they had, in fact, succeeded in withering and killing in them, the whole moral, divine, melodious part of human thought."[89] These men, Lamartine continues, proclaimed: "Calculation and force, cipher and saber, it's all there!" Unfortunately, today's materialists are worse: calculation and money, figures and finance, it's all there.

Confronting GEORGE SOROS

The reaction orchestrated by Viktor Orbán is an insurrection of common sense, the detachment of a star that has become a black hole. Like the circles of hell in Dante's *Inferno*, political orientation goes astray as the level of responsibility moves further away from the people, further away from the earth. This gradation is already perceptible between the countries of Central and Western Europe, and even more so with the Commission. The elite's detachment from the popular interest leads to radicalism but not to secession, in the eyes of Central European populist decision-makers. Excessive dependence precludes any kind of "exit."

---

[89] Preface to *Méditations poétiques*, 1820.

Orbán intends to make his tendency count, alongside others at work on the continent. Systematic opposition to the Commission would mean Hungary shooting itself in the foot. This is why George Soros, one of the leading advocates of the "no border" ideology, soon became the declared *bête noire* of the Hungarian government.[90] The appointment of such an adversary is logical.

George Soros was born in Budapest in 1930 but left his homeland as a teenager at the end of the Second World War. The vast Anglo-Saxon world seemed better suited to him. He studied at the London School of Economics, where he took classes with the Austrian philosopher Karl Popper. In *Open Society and Its Enemies* (1945), Popper theorized about the model of liberal society to which Soros has devoted colossal resources since becoming immensely rich in the 1980s. Such is his financial power that the modest Hungarian émigré has set himself up as a "head of state without a state." The recipe for his prodigious rise is to be found in financial speculation. Nothing has changed since the previous century, when Émile Zola depicted the merciless world of the stock market in *L'argent* (1891). Or rather, history has continued in the same direction: capitalism has expanded, the market has dissolved borders, the free movement of capital and technological innovations have turned the major stock markets into the casinos of the global economy. The ambition, cynicism, and rapacity of George Soros resonate with the rise of the second globalization.[91] The epicenter of this global revolution is New York, the financial capital where Soros has been active since 1956.

With the dollar no longer convertible into gold, other currencies indexed to the dollar are entering a period of unprecedented volatility. This situation opened up infinite possibilities for currency speculation. On September 16, 1992, Soros became "the man who broke the Bank of England," by speculating against the pound. Black Wednesday resulted in

---

[90] "I have to say that an alliance has been formed in Brussels against the opinion of the people. Those taking part in this alliance are the Brussels bureaucrats and their elite, as well as the system that can be called the Soros empire." Viktor Orbán, Tusványos 2017 speech.

[91] A distinction is made between the first globalization (1850-1914), marked by the industrial revolution, and a second globalization heralded by the end of dollar convertibility (announced by President Nixon on August 15, 1971) and the rise of the Internet.

the loss of $3.3 billion for British savers, while the daring stockbroker pocketed $1.1 billion. Soros's fortune lies in this most unphilanthropic predation.

This should be the yardstick by which to judge the philosophy he claims to uphold. Offshore finance, tax havens, and insider trading are the exact measure of the model defended by the advocates of the open society: an Orwellian universe where "enslaved people" call themselves an "open society," where "transparency" guarantees the opacity of the real levers of influence, where "corruption" designates resistance to the corrupters of international finance, and where "freedom" is merely the isolation of the individual from the market, and so on.

In 1984, Soros founded a sprawling network of NGOs dedicated to improving the lot of mankind, an organization that became literally known as the "Open Society Institute" in 1993 and the Open Society Foundations in 2010. Soros earned his stripes as an honest man for this organization's sometimes ill-defined work. By the 2010s, he had grown as old as he is immensely rich and powerful, and in 2023 he handed off leadership to his 37 year-old son Alexander. Soros takes no responsibility for the disastrous consequences of his ideology, far less so than a misguided head of state, and even less so than the bureaucrats of the European Commission. Outside any political or territorial framework, he sums up and embodies globalism, free of any counterweight.

The Open Society Foundations (OSF) are playing an active role in the migration crisis.[92] Let us confine ourselves to the case of one OSF-funded think tank: the European Stability Initiative (ESI).[93] When Angela Merkel declared on German television on October 8 that she had a plan to manage migration, she was careful not to add that this plan had been provided to her four days earlier by the ESI. Indeed, the text, titled "Merkel Plan," is still available on the NGO's website, dating from October 4, 2015. The broad outlines correspond to the position assumed by the German Chancellor and to the agreement negotiated with Turkey between October

---

[92] On September 26, 2015, George Soros personally called for asylum reform via press release on project-syndicate.org.

[93] Details of this lobby's activities can be found in Pierre-Antoine Plaquevent, *Soros et la société ouverte*, 2018, Éditions Le retour aux sources.

2015 and April 2016.[94]

The Hungarian Prime Minister is right to identify Soros as the main adversary of his policies; although he is a cosmopolitan, his Hungarian origins offer a privileged identification bias in the eyes of public opinion. Orbán presented his fellow citizens with the "Soros Plan."[95] After a massive poster campaign, the Orbán administration organized a national consultation. Every citizen was given the opportunity to respond to seven postulates[96] put forward by the government. On the strength of the 2.3 million responses received, in January 2018 the Prime Minister presented a "Stop Soros package," which was adopted after the parliamentary elections on April 8. The renewal of the National Assembly, two-thirds of whose seats had been won by Fidesz, was seen in the rhetoric of the reappointed Prime Minister as a national victory over globalist interests.

---

[94] See esiweb.org.

[95] "There is a Soros plan. It has four points. Mr. Soros wrote it himself, and his empire has published it and begun mobilizing for its execution. The plan calls for several hundred thousand, if not a million, migrants from the Muslim world to enter Europe every year. The second point specifies that each of them will receive 15,000 euros on entering Europe, which the author of the plan will be happy to finance: not insignificant, but secondary. It's not that, it's not the commercial profit that is at the heart of the project, but the fact that we can thus ensure the continuity of the migratory flow. In other words, those who wish to see at least one million migrants arrive each year must maintain the phenomenon, which in our jargon we call the 'pull factor.' The movement must not stop. And if they're spread out, and everyone gets a sum of this magnitude – which, by the way, is more than the average Hungarian annual income – it is clear that there won't be any succession problems. The third point of the Soros plan prescribes that incoming migrants are to be distributed among the countries of Europe on the basis of a compulsory and permanent mechanism. And the fourth, that a European immigration agency should be set up to take over all decision-making powers on migration from the nation-states and place them in the hands of Brussels. This is the Soros plan." Viktor Orbán, Tusványos speech, July 29, 2017.

[96] 1. George Soros is trying to convince Brussels to settle at least a million migrants from Africa and the Middle East on EU territory, including Hungary, every year; 2. George Soros and the Brussels leadership want to succeed in getting EU member states, including Hungary, to dismantle their border protection barriers, so as to open their borders to immigrants; 3. The Soros plan also involves forcing the distribution of the immigrants massing in Western Europe, in particular to the countries of Eastern Europe. Hungary would then also have to contribute; 4. On the basis of the Soros plan, Brussels should force member states, and thus Hungary, to pay 9 million forints (€15,000) in state aid to each migrant; 5. George Soros also wants migrants to receive lighter sentences for their crimes; 6. The aim of the Soros plan is to relegate the language and culture of European countries to the background in order to speed up the integration of illegal immigrants; 7. The Soros plan also aims to initiate political attacks and harsh sanctions against countries opposed to immigration.

This campaign is also a political maneuver. It saturates the public debate and sets Viktor Orbán above partisan political debate. Above all, it demonstrates the responsiveness of the Hungarian state when its capacity for action is no longer constrained by common membership of a political space or by economic interdependence. Finally, this conflict illustrates the inexorable divorce between democracy and liberalism.

On the one hand, there lie the OSF's Soros billions and Pierre Moscovici, who deplored in October 2015[97] that "not enough intellectual and political work has been done on the former communist bloc countries' adherence to European values." On the other hand, there is Orbán's reaction, expressed in light of the unexpected election of Donald Trump as President of the United States in 2016: "What has happened is that reality has shattered ideology. We are returning to reality, which means respecting the opinions of real people and what they think, how they approach these issues – not to educate them, but to accept them as they are, because they are the basis of democracy."[98]

Liberalism: a spectre haunting Europe

A society is only as liberal as its exhaustion. Napoleon's adventures left France drained and disillusioned, as Alfred de Musset poignantly depicted.[99] The imperial comet consumed the sap of old monarchical loyalty. Chateaubriand made no mistake, lamenting the victory of decadent individualism over a sense of duty in Restoration Europe.[100] Beyond the discrediting of nationalist fervor, the result was the decline of all forms of civicmindedness. The new era, ushered in by the beheading of a king, soon led to the renunciation of all that exceeds the pettiness of the individual. Balzac perceived this with his usual acuity when he denounced "the real wounds of our civilization, which, since 1815, has replaced the principle of Honor with the principle of Money."[101] And contractual logic

---

[97] cf. "A refugee doesn't come to Europe to leave again." Interview published in *Le Point*, October 26, 2015.
[98] Interview by Peter Foster for the *Daily Telegraph*, November 11, 2016.
[99] Alfred de Musset, *La confession d'un enfant du siècle*, 1836.
[100] François-René de Chateaubriand, *De la morale des intérêts et de la morale des devoirs*, *Le Conservateur*, December 5, 1818.
[101] Honoré de Balzac, *Melmoth réconcilié*, 1835.

spread over the ruins: the desert grows.[102]

Whether a resounding defeat or ideological disavowal, national destruction is always met by disintegration into relativism, skepticism, egotism. The result of this general decline is a more direct face-off between the isolated individual and the two powers at work in the contemporary world: the market and the state. Abandoned to this cruel fate, each generation pretends to emancipate itself from servitude while "the world unravels," to use Albert Camus's eloquent expression.[103]

The liberal state recognizes only individuals and implements equality between them. In the same effort to standardize, it organizes the competition of all against all, i.e. the equality of individuals before the market. For beyond the authorized stirrings of blossoming nationalism, only "gentle commerce"[104] connects people in a society emancipated from the shackles of yesteryear.

Society is inexorably falling apart, plunged into "the icy waters of selfish calculation." Marxism was a historical response to the dysfunctions of the liberal state; it was unable to remedy them, as it was merely a shaping of industrial society – and by no means an overcoming of its contradictions. Communism attempts to modify the relations of production in order to achieve individual equality despite the market. But it shares with liberalism the same individualistic and universalist foundations, the same radical hostility to tradition, the same contempt for the filial and spiritual roots of the social order. Liberalism and socialism are part of the same exhaustion of civilization. As for nationalism, it disappears correlatively with the decline of the citizen as consumer. If a social force maintains or regains a foothold in a common culture, it is demonized for opposing the plenitude of the undifferentiated individual. Liberal logic, instituted to protect people from conflict, is then deployed in a totalitarian fashion to defeat all resistance to the state and the market.

*

---

[102] Reference to Friedrich Nietzsche's formula denouncing the diminishment of man, *Thus Spoke Zarathustra*, IV, "Among the Daughters of the Desert," § 2.
[103] In his acceptance speech for the Nobel Prize for Literature, 1957.
[104] Allusion to Montesquieu's famous formula, *De l'esprit des lois*, Livre XX, Chapitre 1, 1748.

Beyond the political ups and downs of the modern age, the only positive driving force behind the evolution of liberal society is money: the standard and horizon of all human activity. Gentle commerce as a privileged link between individuals leads to the unlimited power of the economy: at the end of the slide, the social contract seems to be established on the tacit promise of increased economic growth. Man is seen as nothing more than an economic agent, nature as an exploitable resource, and the country as a hotel open to anything that can increase the production of wealth. In this lamentable abasement is reflected the fall of all that is great, noble and divine.

Liberalism can only be defined by default. Nietzsche evokes in a remarkably limpid and bitter page how its institutions are only worth as much as we aspire to them without knowing them:

> The value of a thing sometimes lies not in what you gain by getting it, but in what you pay for it – in what it costs. Let me give you an example. Liberal institutions cease to be liberal as soon as they are acquired: there is nothing more fundamentally harmful to freedom than liberal institutions. It's well known what they lead to: they undermine the will to power, they level the mountain and the valley, they make people small, cowardly and greedy for pleasure – the triumph of the herd accompanies them every time. Liberalism: in other words, dumbing down by herds ... The same institutions, as long as you have to fight for them, have quite different consequences; they then promote, in a powerful way, the development of freedom.[105]

---

[105] Friedrich Nietzsche, *Twilight of the Idols*, X, § 38, 1888.

IX.

The face of theater is changing

"Political correctness" frames the state as a secular religion. Democracy is subordinated to it, so much so that the electoral game often seems like a carnival at the foot of the throne: opponents reinforce the system with their assault rather than undermine it. But events since 2015 have accelerated the delegitimization of the dominant ideology, which seems less an expression of order than the ferment of chaos. Ideological uncertainty opens up the prospect of political recomposition to the advantage of popular aspirations. This is what we call populism.

Of course, the situation varies from one EU country to another. A constantly evolving typology classifies member states into two families. Some are more aligned than alienated, i.e. suffering under the liberal fetters and loyal out of necessity (often recent or small countries); others are as much – or more – alienated than aligned, i.e. promoters of the headlong rush assumed by Brussels. Since 2010, Hungary and then Poland, with the Czech Republic, Slovakia and other countries to follow, have been rebuilding their states on illiberal foundations: an undeniable development in the EU of 2020, proof that the political landscape is diversifying despite the constraints of the Lisbon Treaty.

2016-2020: Western marginalization and national room for maneuver

The extra-EU environment is evolving. It even expanded to include the United Kingdom, which left in 2019 and appears prepared to stay out, even under the new Labour government elected in 2024. Perhaps history was forced by the proven bad blood between David Cameron and Jean-Claude Juncker. Exasperated by dysfunctional European integration, the British government decided to back up its demands with a solid democratic plebiscite: its people chose to leave in 2016 through "Brexit." The day before the vote, Viktor Orbán had announced his support for Remain in an op-ed published in the *Times*: in his eyes, the English voice counted in the European concert. Nevertheless, the UK returned to its island destiny, without this break-up remedying its slow internal decomposition and, indeed, becoming the subject of considerable popular regret according to post-Brexit opinion polls. The EU has been deprived of a leading country, without this loss shaking the dogmas that caused it. In any case, the difficulties of concluding Brexit underline the ambiguities of the European project rather than its virtues. Free-trade agreements signed with Canada[106] and Mercosur[107] on the one hand, and the difficulty of organizing the continuation of our open trade relations with the United Kingdom on the other suggest that free trade is merely a means of organizing interdependence, itself a vector of impotence.

*

Since 1990, the American metropole has been extending its orbit farther and farther to the east, draped in the role of a guarantor of freedom. Central Europe served as a stepping stone to the Russian world. Both the Obama and Biden administrations regularly attacked the Hungarian government, accusing it of departing from liberal norms, so much so that in 2012 Hillary Clinton, then Secretary of State, wrote an open letter to Viktor Orbán to set him straight.[108] In the context of the 2016 election campaign, in which Clinton was the Democratic nominee, her husband, former president Bill Clinton, declared that "Hungary and Poland have decided that democracy is too much trouble, so they want Putin-style rule."[109] János Lázár, head of Orbán's office, retorted that "Barack Obama, backed by Clinton and Soros, is working to fill Europe with migrants."[110] This antagonism explains the Hungarian Prime Minister's support for the

---

[106] Comprehensive Economic and Trade Agreement (CETA), signed on October 30, 2016; partial and provisional adoption on September 21, 2017.
[107] EU-Mercosur Treaty, signed on June 28, 2019.
[108] Letter dated November 23, 2011.
[109] At a Democratic rally in New Jersey, May 13, 2016.
[110] Communication dated May 19, 2016.

ebullient outsider Donald Trump,[111] whom he recently hailed as "the only man who can save Western civilization."

Europe's migration crisis spurred the American debate on illegal immigration, and it was on the strength of his claim that Trump would start building a wall on the Mexican border and use economic diplomacy to secure Mexican border policing. The unlikely outcome of the election on November 8, 2016, brought deep relief in Budapest. "Democracy is still alive," Orbán communicated on social networks in the early hours of the morning. He was the first head of government to congratulate Trump on his victory. This amity forged at a distance continues. On May 13, 2019, Donald Trump welcomed Orbán to the White House with open arms and began a friendly relationship that continued through the 2024 presidential election campaign, when Orbán visited Trump at his Mar-a-Lago residence in Palm Beach, Florida.

The rejection of the same exacerbated liberalism, which the United States has drunk to the dregs and which Central Europe rejects, makes for an alliance of circumstance.[112] In so doing, Donald Trump is playing a risky game: he is reinforcing the Central European countries in their own affirmation of the "our nation first" leitmotiv, without actually turning them away from the German partnership, or, in Hungary's case, continental partnerships of all kinds.

---

[111] In his Tusványos speech on July 26, 2016, Viktor Orbán described Donald Trump as a "courageous candidate" and claimed that his election would be good news for Europe.

[112] Donald Trump's speech in Warsaw, delivered on July 7, 2017, was his first major international address, testifying to an undeniable convergence with Central European patriotism: "The history of Poland is the history of a people who have never been broken and who have never forgotten who they are. And I am here today, not only to visit an old ally, but also to stand with those who fight and seek freedom, and who give the world an example of courage in defense of our civilization. America, Poland and the nations of Europe share the values of individual freedom and sovereignty. We must rise together to challenge the forces that come from within or without, from south or west, and that threaten these values, that harm our culture, our faith and our traditions that make us who we are. What we have inherited from our ancestors has never existed before us to this degree, and if we fail to preserve it, it will never exist again in the future. So we cannot fail. The fundamental question of our time is whether the West has the will to survive. Do we have the confidence in our values to defend them at all costs? Do we have enough respect for our citizens to protect our borders? Do we have the desire and courage to defend our civilization against those who subvert and destroy it? Poland cannot be destroyed, I declare to the world today. The West will never, ever be broken. Our values will triumph."

The American empire's regard for the distant reaches of the West has hardly changed. But China's expansion into the Pacific has begun to reshape Uncle Sam's priorities. Brexit also removed the EU's Anglo-Saxon component, in a reversal of what Charles de Gaulle feared UK membership – which he twice vetoed – would bring in. Brussels[113] took advantage of Donald Trump's election, and has been using his 2024 reelection campaign, to draw a distinction between "the good United States" and "the dubious Trump-led Republican Party" in order to undo its master's chain in the uncertain context of deglobalization. This is a mimetic reaction to Donald Trump's isolationism, and many believe it is a profound recomposition of the American right into a national conservative movement. The return of the Democrats to the White House in 2021 could not conceal the obvious: Europe and North America share fewer and fewer interests.

The atmosphere of "soft civil war" in the USA and the UK's Brexit trauma prove that point: the Anglo-Saxon world is plunging into self-inflicted doubt and less capable to lead. Seen from continental Europe, this development conceals an opportunity: distancing ourselves from the Anglo-Saxons breaks Western universalism from within. Contrary to the obsessive universalism of Brussels, a political and identity-based clarification is emerging: how can we integrate Turkey into the EU when we are separating from England?

*

The decomposition of the Western order accelerated in 2020, with the Covid-19 epidemic. The management of the crisis exposed the West's failings and insecurities, particularly amid new evidence suggesting that the virus was manufactured in a Chinese laboratory. In 1918 and 1945, order was established: now we have the impression of inexorable decomposition, with intangible forces, rising challenges, and state and non-state actors contributing to decay. In this context, organized nuclei can become centers of influence.

Viktor Orbán took swift action to ensure the safety of the Hungarian population. On March 11, 2020, article 53 of the Basic Law was activated,

---

[113] Or more precisely: German commercial interests.

establishing a "state of danger" for a period of fifteen days. This authorized the government to legislate by emergency decree in areas of public health. The opposition immediately denounced this as a coup d'état, and the Prime Minister countered with a political maneuver. Even before the expiration of the two-week state of emergency, which could be extended with parliamentary approval, the government requested an early extension, requiring the vote of fourth-fifth of deputies. Trapped in its anti-government rhetoric, the disparate third of opposition MPs refused. Orbán lost nothing in substance, as the two-thirds majority of the assembly effectively renewed the state of emergency on March 30.[114] The same cannot be said of the parties united against Fidesz: unable to take the general interest into account, locked into a sterile role of war against the government, they give the impression of echoing malign recriminations. These were unleashed with unprecedented violence in the spring of 2020. Hungary simply became a dictatorship, according to the headlines. Orbán was summoned by the European Parliament on May 14 to explain himself during a debate – the tenth since 2010 – on Hungary's alleged excesses. He refused to attend, arguing that the state of emergency was taking up his time and that the Minister of Justice, Judith Varga, was perfectly qualified to represent him. But Parliament refused to receive her, and the representative of an EU government was reduced to publishing her speech on social media. She denounced the attacks on a member state at the height of an unprecedented crisis as a "historic betrayal of the European family." So much so that, according to Judith Varga, "the [European] parliament is not the solution, it is part of the problem." The Commission agreed with Hungary, acknowledging that no abuse of power or constitutional infringement has been committed. This reality did not prevented MEPs on the left of the Chamber from calling for Hungary to be deprived of future European funds, ironically including those intended to combat the pandemic. Financial strangulation seems to be the ultimate form of coercion that Brussels employs, in the event of a dispute with a member state. The conditionality of European funds bears witness to coercive

---

[114] In accordance with paragraph 4 of article 53 of the Basic Law, the state of danger in Hungary ended when the epidemic no longer required exceptional measures, by a vote of Parliament on June 16.

hostility inspired by ideology. It strikes at recalcitrant countries according to criteria other than economic ones: in return, the EU exposes itself to a veritable rebellion.

In a peculiar inversion, incantatory complaints are the prerogative of liberals, and effective action that of national conservatives. The state of emergency assumed by Orbán does not imply strict confinement.

In the face of this honorable achievement, how are we to understand Western aggression, which is as incapable of discussion as it is of winning? History is accelerating, giving the illiberal state the opportunity to illustrate its viability and regularity. While attacks on Hungary have become more passionate, this does not mean that the balance of power has shifted in favor of the liberals. Quite the contrary, in fact. The more the Western system falls into trouble, the more imperative it is to find an alternative model. It is this unbreathable wind of freedom that is disempowering the liberals.

2019: the challenges of an electoral transformation

The purpose of European integration is not to harmoniously secure the space in which nations exercise their sovereignty, but to protect them from themselves: in other words, to undo them. And yet, national determinism drives the Europe of Brussels. To understand the EU, we need to observe the workings within the bureaucracy.

The European Union is essentially an association of member states that share a single market, with its own control tower: the European Commission. The Union is defined as *sui generi*. In other words, as a whole exceeding the sum of its parts. But undeniably, the "exit" of all or even some members would remove the whole. Brexit was a reminder of the fragility of any unitary framework in Europe, all the more so as the activation of the blocking minority can hamper the functioning of the institutions at any time.

Despite the Commission's prerogatives, the real power in the EU lies with the Council and the majority that emerges from it. There are two complementary institutions: the European Council, which brings together the Heads of State, appoints the President of the European Commission and sets the Union's general political agenda; and the Council of the EU, which co-legislates with the Parliament, representing the governments of the Member States. Some votes require unanimity, others a qualified majority. The latter requires the favorable vote of 55% of member states, representing 65% of the EU population. Until November 1, 2014, a weighting system distributed 260 points.[115] The blocking minority stood at 93. The sum of the votes of the four countries of the Visegrád group is 58 points: as much as the Franco-German couple, but too few to derail decisions adopted under the ordinary procedure. What's more, the current system only requires the veto of four countries to constitute a blocking minority, representing at least 35% of the EU population, far more than the 14.25% constituted by the V4. A proper blocking vote would therefore require the support of large countries such as Italy and Spain or the enlargement of the opposition front to include a considerable number of smaller countries.

However, nothing prevents a country from unilaterally remedying an emergency situation by suspending the application of Community legislation. But the dissident state must arm itself with popular support and its best legal minds. For a long time, giving up and falling into line was easier until the controversy surrounding migrant quotas changed things. Faced with the united refusal of the Central European countries, the Juncker Commission gave in despite a decision adopted by a large majority in the Council.

The European framework has tried to cover the national fact with a star-spangled flag, but that hardly eliminates it. It can even be said that the law of the strongest prevails in today's Europe without much nuance. The rule of law conceals it more than it limits it. The decisive years that the EU is going through bear the poisoned mark of these maneuvers in the name of the rule of law; to anticipate their continuation, we need to return to the balance of power resulting from the 2019 European elections.

---

[115] The weight of each member state offered a schematic overview of the inter-state balance of power in the EU: 29 votes for Germany, France, the UK and Italy; 27 for Spain and Poland; 14 for Romania and 13 for the Netherlands; 12 for Greece, the Czech Republic, Hungary, Portugal, and Belgium; 10 for Sweden, Austria, and Bulgaria; 7 for Slovakia, Denmark, Finland, Lithuania, Croatia, and Ireland; 4 for Latvia, Slovenia, Estonia, Cyprus, and Luxembourg; 3 for Malta.

*

The relative exhaustion of the Carolingian core did not prevent the European Titanic from arriving safely in port at the May 2019 elections and undergoing a regulatory crew change. The extraordinary European Council from June 30 to July 2, 2019, rendered the state of play in the EU at the dawn of the new term. The agenda consisted precisely of the appointment of the various holders of key Union posts.[116] Unlike the same exercise in 2014, nothing is going according to plan. The *Spitzenkandidat* system was written off:[117] many member states were reluctant to accept this type of selection, which consecrated the candidate that the German CDU succeeded in imposing on the EPP. Angela Merkel had anticipated this difficulty. Ahead of the Council, at the G7 meeting in Osaka, she agreed with her French counterpart to support the Dutch Socialist candidate Frans Timmermans. This breach with her political family in the name of the *Spitzenkandidat's* federalist logic caused an outcry in the EPP at the instigation of Orbán.[118] Merkel was no longer in a position to lay down the law, either in her party or in the Council. Emmanuel Macron conveniently shunned his ally, for one main reason: Germany's refusal to approve transnational lists for the European elections had compromised the logic of the *Spitzenkandidat*, in his view. The federalists were caught in their own trap. The Council was bogged down for two days. In the end, it chose Ursula von der Leyen, a member of the CDU and Minister of Defense in the German federal government. It was not quite back to square one: the blocking minority actually worked in the sense that it can hinder any headlong rush and opens up new prospects for the populist tendencies at work on the continent. The same principle emerged in 2024, when

---

[116] The Presidency of the EU Commission and Council, the High Representative for Foreign Policy and the Presidency of the ECB.

[117] Since 2014, there has been a provision for candidates for the Commission presidency to be the heads of lists of European political parties in elections; this is to reinforce the supranational dimension of the ballot. However, this provision does not appear in the Treaties. Logically, Jean-Claude Juncker's heir at the head of the European Commission should have been the EPP's *Spitzenkandidat*, Manfred Weber.

[118] On the very day of the Council meeting, the Hungarian Prime Minister sent a letter, albeit suspended from the EPP, to its President Joseph Daul, alerting him to the dangers of the "Timmermans option;" he then took the initiative of a counter-offensive at the head of the other EPP heads of state.

European elections returned an even stronger presence for the nationalist right, forcing von der Leyen to squeak through to a renewal of her mandate by an even slimmer margin. The illegible nature of European party structures, however, is another indication of the system's exhaustion: the purist Emmanuel Macron has had to contend in his parliamentary group, Renew Europe, with the Czech populists of ANO 2011, and the highly pragmatic Spaniards of Ciudadanos,[119] along with the right in his own country, which as of 2024 is the largest party in both its EU parliamentary delegation and France's National Assembly.

Given the imbroglio of institutional Europe, we must look to the situation of the continent's three main countries, Germany, France and Italy, to find favorable resonances for Hungary's illiberal agenda - and sketch out the new European deal.

Germany, a power for nothing?

Germany's dominance of the continent does not preclude deep internal divisions, especially since Chancellor Angela Merkel employed the diligent conservative machine that is the CDU in the service of a revolutionary migration policy. This contradiction added to the confusion that reigns in the German political landscape. It's worth remembering that, while Angela Merkel was installed in the Chancellery in 2005, she seized the presidency of the CDU as early as 2000. The party congress in December 2018 provided an opportunity for a power transfer. Runner-up Annegret Kramp-Karrenbauer narrowly defeated Friedrich Merz, who favored a break with the centrist line he had taken until then.

This rise was not enough to ensure the stature of the runner-up, who came up against the hostility of the media and was soon at loggerheads with the Chancellor herself. After two years of mixed experience, the party came under the presidency of Armin Laschet. This lackluster politician led the center-right to a historic defeat in the federal elections on September 26, 2021, losing nine points compared to the previous elections. The Merkel era came to a screeching halt, with the nationalist right continuing

---

[119] Ciudadanos is a Spanish unionist and liberal party, and an unclassifiable one at that. Its alliance in Andalusia with Vox, in December 2018, broke the "republican arc" that Emmanuel Macron intended to impose on his allies.

to make impressive gains in local and regional elections.

But the decline goes back a long way: as soon as the migrant crisis broke out, Merkel embarked upon a period of turbulence, never to return. In 2017, the CDU/CSU had already lost 8.5 points compared to 2013, achieving its worst score since 1949. The AfD, with 12% of the vote, suddenly became a force in the Bundestag. A score that is both unprecedented and meager if we consider that only this party assumes a radical critique of the migration policy followed since 2015. This positioning disqualified the AfD from taking part in a coalition. Angela Merkel navigated for many months before sealing an alliance in February 2018 with the SPD,[120] the country's second largest party, albeit also in disarray.

Across Germany, internal fractures have become more pronounced. The former East Germany[121] on the one hand, and Bavaria,[122] on the other, cultivate an identity distinct from the Rhine. If the status quo holds, it will be because the economy is the key, and it's holding its own – so far and just barely. Merkel's decline seems to be incubating explosive contradictions; a mixture of coldness, brutality, and incompetence characterizes Germany today. The country's neutralization has continued to worsen since the parliamentary elections of 2021 and the formation of a coalition dominated by the Social Democrats.

And yet, Germany occupies first place in the European Union. Through its trade surplus, the euro and its ascendancy in European institutions, even more than through its demographic weight and central geographical location. The Federal Republic extends throughout the German-speaking world, from the Benelux countries to Austria, and from there to the whole of Europe. This trend can be explained as a resurgence: that of a central consciousness, if not an imperial atavism. The continent's economic path is a product of German ordo-liberalism. The austerity

---

[120] Angela Merkel begins her fourth term of office on March 14.

[121] The six former East German Länder, with the exception of Berlin, are largely turning to the AfD, to the detriment not only of the CDU, but also of the far left (Die Linke) and the Social Democrats (SPD).

[122] Ahead of the Bavarian Landtag elections on October 14, 2018, tensions are running high between the CDU and CSU. And with good reason, the maintenance of the historic alliance with the federal sister party is resulting in a 10-point drop compared to the 2013 ballot.

imposed on Greece largely at Germany's behest since 2008 is a clear illustration of this.

In addition to this economic pressure, German ascendancy is growing politically, as the fall of the Austrian government in 2019 suggested. On May 17, a shock video spread simultaneously through the German media *Der Spiegel* and *Süddeutsche Zeitung* and around the world. The video shows Heinz-Christian Strache[123] compromising himself with a young woman claiming to be the niece of a Russian oligarch. In particular, the story concerns the oligarch's takeover of the *Kronen Zeitung, a* large-circulation periodical, in return for the promise of public contracts. The scandal hits the FPÖ right in the guts, just a few days before the European elections. A fearsome, long-prepared frame-up, the video was shot in Ibiza, in a house rented by German television, in July 2017 – six months before the formation of an FPÖ-ÖVP coalition in Vienna and in the wake of elections marked by identity and security concerns. The manipulation of Johann Gudenus[124] required months of planning and considerable resources to make the usurpation of an oligarch plausible. No one has been able to uncover the instigator of the plot; the trail stops at a lawyer of Iranian origin, Ramin Mirfakhrai, who is said to have commissioned the video: everything leads us to believe that he may be a figurehead for a larger cabal

Strache resigned the day after the scandal and Chancellor Sebastian Kurz announced early elections the day after. Austria acts as a bridge between Central Europe, Italy, and Southern and Eastern Germany. A group whose coalition could call into question the political line imperturbably followed by Berlin.

The conservative press in Hungary was not afraid to talk of a second Anschluss. Needless to say, the conservative camps in Germany and Hungary do not reflect the same reality. The chasm separating "Christian democracy" in these two countries created a rift between Fidesz and the

---

[123] Heinz-Christian Strache is an important populist figure in Austria: architect of the revival of the Freiheitliche Partei Österreichs (FPÖ), which he chaired from 2005 to 2019, and Vice-Chancellor of Austria from December 2017 to May 2019.

[124] FPÖ executive in charge of relations with the Slavic world. After the electoral success of October 2017, he became head of the FPÖ group in the Austrian Parliament; he resigned from all his political functions following *Ibizagate*.

EPP. This was because the latter is also subject to the dominant influence of its German component: the CDU. Belonging to Europe's largest political family was now only a secondary asset for Viktor Orbán, much less important than his undeniable legitimacy on national soil and in national institutions, and all the more so as the Polish PiS was keen to welcome its Hungarian friends into the European Conservatives and Reformists (ECR). Paradoxically, the Hungarians' detachment from their exclusion complicated the task of the EPP's governing bodies. All efforts have been focused on the famous Sargentini report, the adoption of which was supposed to depict the illiberal drift with infamy. Far from making amends, Fidesz campaigned for the 2019 European elections by associating Jean-Claude Juncker and George Soros on billboards across the country. Brussels and Berlin fulminated, but plans for Hungary's exclusion changed to a unanimous suspension[125] in order to postpone the final decision until after the European elections. However, Orbán left with a vacation assignment: to fill in a questionnaire from the European party authorities responsible for deciding his fate. At the beginning of July, he handed in the questionnaire. The direct, even caustic tone of the letter illustrates the extent to which Orbán does not beg to keep his political party together. Indeed, to dismiss it would be to take on the responsibility of starting a process of disintegration of the European Right, an option objectively detrimental to the interests of the CDU.[126] When Fidesz officially announced its departure from the EPP on March 18, 2021, it formalized a separation that had already been assumed. It also signaled the collapse of the center-right and the beginnings of a European national conservative alternative.

France between inertia and aggiornamento

The Anglo-Saxon world is outside Europe, but France is at its heart.

---

[125] March 20, 2019, at the EPP Political Assembly.

[126] The Covid-19 pandemic reinforced this trend. On April 3, 2020, EPP Secretary General Antonio López-Istúriz White sent an alarming missive to the Hungarian Prime Minister, regarding the state of danger decreed in connection with the pandemic. Orbán replied scathingly: "I don't have time for this." Yet on September 28, 2020, EPP President Donald Tusk conceded that it was impossible to exclude Fidesz from its ranks: "Let's not kid ourselves: not everyone rejects Viktor Orbán's way of thinking."

The sensible question coming from France may not be whether or not it belongs to the European entity of the moment, but how it defines the latter according to its decisive contribution to it. The "austerity turn" in France dates back to 1983. Jacques Delors became head of the European Commission in 1985 to prepare the Single European Act and the Maastricht Treaty, the crucible of neo-liberalism in force in the EU today.

Schematically, Germany is extending its economic sway into an open France, but Paris is spreading its ideas with undeniable power across the Rhine, and from there to the whole of Europe. In this respect, the election of Emmanuel Macron as President of the Republic in May 2017 marked a turning point. The overhaul of the EU became the priority issue in French politics. Macron's "at the same time"[127] policy has led him to take on contradictory positions, from hackneyed idealism to jarring pragmatism.

From the start of his first presidential campaign, Macron anticipated the Manichean struggle that would pit him against the nationalist right in France – known since 2018 as the Rassemblement National. Macron's attacks on Poland caused the first diplomatic incident. On September 26, 2017, the French president gave a wide-ranging speech at the Sorbonne pleading for the relaunch of European integration as a virtuous project capable of regaining the upper hand over the evil fairies of the century: "nationalism, identitarianism, protectionism." He asserted: "They claim to be legitimate because they cynically exploit people's fears. For too long, we have ignored their power." This demonization of the national interest aroused little enthusiasm among his counterparts across the continent. In Central Europe, it frankly irritated those who heard him, all the more since these remarks seemed to confirm the French President's attempt to divide the Visegrád group. Such rhetoric revealed a certain nationalism, pitting a civilization of good against barbarians incapable of recognizing it: this divisive stance hardly saw any inflection until the 2019 European elections, and thereafter expanded in 2024. All the more so as the European scene remained dead calm during the long months of institutional crisis in Germany. Finally, in the spring of 2018, Macron re-

---

[127] The "*en même temps*" (at the same time) is a recurrent element of the French President's vocabulary, enabling him to combine contradictory elements in order to propose a political synthesis.

entered the fray with an address to the European Parliament on April 17 and a bilateral meeting with the German Chancellor in Berlin two days later. In Strasbourg, Jean-Claude Juncker and Manfred Weber[128] lectured the French president on the need to reach agreement with 27 members rather than two. Merkel politely sidestepped her counterpart's enthusiastic proposal to overhaul the EU.

There are two things that the French president can be credited with in 2018: the Meseberg Declaration[129] and the Treaty of Aachen.[130] The first was a Franco-German declaration of intent endorsing the general direction that the two powers intend to impose on the EU. The second was a friendship treaty outlining the convergence of the two countries in all areas, notably defense and foreign policy. The serious flaw in this convergence lies in the denial that underpins it. Leaning on each other, the two countries are disintegrating together instead of courageously addressing their internal weaknesses either separately or in common. Germany devotes itself to its industrial power, which seems to take the place of a collective identity or at least as an indisputable factor of power. France, on the other hand, only exports ideological obstinacy, a contribution that is all the less national for its globalist ideology.

From this point of view, Macron has expressed the dominant tendency of the French elite. They disdain playing France's role. Such was the case of Bruno Le Maire, France's Minister of the Economy and Finance, who in 2018 published an essay on the unitary future of the continent.[131] Le Maire professed desired changes rather than contributing directly to them through the health of the national economy for which he was responsible. Bruno Le Maire conjectured that "European sovereignty will be twofold. It will be national *and* Community, Community *and* national."[132] And elsewhere: "sovereignty will be of a different kind from all the others we know ... it will build on national sovereignties, it will not erase them." But

---

[128] Member of the Bavarian CSU and Chairman of the EPP parliamentary group.

[129] Signed on June 19, 2018.

[130] Signed on January 22, 2019, 56 years to the day after the Élysée Treaty was signed by Charles de Gaulle and Konrad Adenauer. The former was a treaty of "reconciliation," the latter is intended to be a treaty of "convergence."

[131] Bruno Le Maire, *Le nouvel empire*, Gallimard, 2018.

[132] Ibid.

intellectual zeal could not make up for political laziness. In the France of
Macron's movement, called "Renaissance" since 2022, Europe would find
no national sovereignty on which to rely: already transfigured in Europe,
it is no longer there[133] even while each nation remains in its place. This
unbridled idealism is not gratuitous. Illusion devours reality. The gap
between the pretensions of the one and the anemia of the other leads to the
breaking point. The right-wing protest actions and votes are a symptom of
this. France is proposing to Europe a path with itself in the vanguard, and
which makes a mockery of Europe's peoples and history. As a last resort,
it will be up to the French people to deny this post-national path, in order
to render it obsolete in Europe. In the 2024 elections, they took a powerful
step in that direction.

On an essential subject: defense and the geopolitical orientation of the
continent, the French position evolved from the summer of 2019. On
August 19, Macron received Vladimir Putin to calm relations with Russia
against the backdrop of the resolution of the Ukrainian conflict. On August
27, the French President drove the point home at his annual conference
with ambassadors. Macron did not shy away from his characteristic "at the
same time" approach. With unprecedented frankness, he spoke of the
emergence of "state-civilizations" that are rethinking and "redefining the
political imaginary." He defended a "European civilization project"
implicitly dissociated from the United States. On November 7, the
Economist published an explosive interview with the French President.
The headline "NATO is brain-dead" summed up the content of the
interview. The situation is as clear as it is worrying. Europe is discovering
itself as a rich suburb in decline, in which the Americans no longer
consider it profitable to invest. Meanwhile, the signals sent to Ukraine
were disastrous, with Joe Biden publicly saying he would not resist a
"minor" Russian incursion just before the 2022 invasion and the Baltic
states and Poles clearly feeling vulnerable amid right-wing American
threats to NATO. Precisely in this respect, Macron confided "Things are
moving forward. I'm not saying that everyone is falling into line. I had a

---

[133] So much so, that the same swaggering, domineering instinct seems to inspire both
federalists and secessionist Frexit advocates: one intends to enslave the EU, the other to
annihilate it.

very long discussion with Viktor Orbán on this subject. He's quite close to our views and has a key intellectual and political role within the Visegrád group, which is important." Macron received Orbán at the Elysée Palace on October 11, 2019, for a long and cordial meeting. At that time, the two leaders had just suffered a slap in the face from the European Parliament, rejecting the French and Hungarian candidates for the post of European Commissioner. Faced with Berlin's mixture of inertia and hegemony, an unprecedented partnership seemed to be taking shape between Paris and Budapest, even though Macron would later deal with his domestic left to check the advance of national conservatives in his own country.

The populist leaven in Italy

Populist dynamism has also strengthened in Italy, which had been slipping since the economic crisis of 2008. The boot has been subjected to all kinds of oligarchic smoke and mirrors, from the government of experts to Matteo Renzi's New Left. But austerity measures accomplished nothing. As the Eurozone's third-largest economy after Germany and France, and a major industrial power, Italy is following the same path as Greece, while immigration was pouring in across the Mediterranean. The political choices made in Central Europe, however, served as a powerful model for Italy.

The Italian slump initially favored the ascendancy of two populist forces: the Five-Star Movement (M5S) founded by Beppe Grillo on the one hand, and the regionalist party *Lega Nord*, renamed *Lega* in 2017, on the other. This transformation, assumed by Matteo Salvini, the party's federal secretary since 2013, offered the Lega the national scope it lacked. Against this backdrop, the Italian general election of March 4, 2018 saw the left-wing populists of the M5S come out on top with 32% of the vote. The right-wing coalition, however, garnered 37% of the vote.[134] Lengthy negotiations led to a historic agreement between populists of the left and right: Guiseppe Conte, an independent jurist, presided over the National Council in which Luigi Di Maio and Matteo Salvini, heads of the M5S and Lega, respectively, sat as vice-presidents.

---

[134] 17% for Lega, 14% for Forza Italia, and 6% for Fratelli d'Italia.

The balance of power shifted in favor of the Lega and its leader. The fragile agreement made it impossible to adopt an alternative political line. The position of Minister of the Interior served as a platform for Matteo Salvini. The muscular management of illegal immigration largely contributed to his aura, even if it did not solve the problem. On August 29, 2018, Orbán's visit to Milan sealed an alliance that has continued ever since. In May 2019, the Lega triumphed in the European elections with almost 35% of the vote. Matteo Salvini captured the hearts of Italians but remained trapped in an incapacitating coalition. In August, he called for new elections. But the populists on the left preferred to associate the Democratic Party with power rather than return the vote to the ballot box. The leader of the Lega, now back in opposition, testified to the endurance of Italian populism but ultimately yielded to the dynamism of new Fratelli d'Italia party led by Georgia Meloni while the M5S faded into the background. In 2022, Meloni became prime minister of the most right-wing government in Italy since Mussolini, with FdI standing at the head of a coalition that agreed to support the leader of its largest party for the top office. While she has softened some of her positions on Europe for tactical reasons, her migration policy has been highly effective in reducing numbers and preventing resettlement.

*

Combined with the rapid evolution of Central Europe, the antagonistic movements of the great nations augur many new perspectives: time is speeding up. In a Union of contrasts and divisions, the cohabitation of nation-states seems difficult. National polycentrism lends real dynamism to the whole.

X.

Towards a new age of order

In an increasingly troubled international context, the internal recomposition of Europe and its nations is becoming even more urgent. The essential issue is to distinguish the political framework from the ideology that infects it in order to reappropriate the former through more fruitful popular aspirations, but also to provide these confused trends with theoretical content and realistic ambition. This effort, now being spearheaded by Viktor Orbán's Hungary, aims first and foremost to make nations masters of their own destiny. It also aims to build a viable European order.

Since Maastricht, the EU has undeniably had a historic role to play: serving as a bias for liberal globalism in Europe. And to bring its own normative weight to bear on the unification of the world market. As the force of popular gravity can only be exerted through the intermediary of nations, the EU's framework and ideology are intimately linked. From this point of view, Brussels is nothing but a factor in the dislocation of borders, limits, and cultures for the benefit of capital.

But the European framework is not strictly superimposed on ideological evil. Below, we have seen how ideology dominates member states, whereas society still offers a popular – albeit partial and residual – foundation. From above, Europe as a whole integrates itself into the Western world – indeed, into the "developed world" – subject to the same logic. The changes underway in London and Washington are limited to adjustments of Anglo-Saxon capitalism, rather than its overcoming. From an illiberal point of view, abolishing the European project is tantamount to sacrificing a scapegoat.

The metamorphoses of the void

The EU claims a role in history by placing itself as the culmination of a necessary evolution. But this federalist self-image is abusive. They are ruining the civilization of which they see themselves as the continuation, or even as the crowning glory. But Brussels is too small to digest Europe: Hungary's rise is enough to give it heartburn, and Poland's assertiveness triggered a liver ulcer.

To adhere to any "idea of Europe" is to recognize a supranational unitary principle. If it's liberalism, it doesn't distinguish Europe: it dissolves it. In the 2020s, liberalism is already no longer a unitary principle within the continent, since Central Europe has broken from it. More to the point, the ruling elite is detaching itself from the national community as well.

The EU is viable because it at least nominally escapes its ideologues: it poses as a unitary framework of civilization, a resurgence of the *Respublica Christiana*, a continuation of Rome. Such an illustrious heritage cannot be abandoned to the masters of the day. So, by drowning Europe in historical amnesia and migratory floods, the EU is sawing off the branch on which it is sitting. The rising tide is working to ensure that the wavering branch topples the EU before turning green again. Or, to use another metaphor, let the prevailing wind give way to other winds to bring the ship into port.

*

A more theoretical consideration is in order here. Placed under the iron rule of the State and European institutions, are peoples in a protective framework or in a rut? Answer: both, inseparably. No one, it may seem, can escape the political order. There is nothing outside it. This awareness makes us responsible, for any secession is an abandonment of post.

The people are not the state, but they exist politically within its binding framework. Nations are not the EU, but they are largely situated in the international political space vis-à-vis this *sui generis* framework. The people must be willing in the face of the state: they support it by containing its hold. And in so doing, the entire body politic is maintained. By the same token, nations must express their will in the face of the EU – and not against it – in order to support European unity by containing it, and thus consolidate a viable continental order.[135] Just as there is no outside, there is no end. It is not so much a question of envisaging a great evening as of honorably following the path that destiny has set before us, to give back to our children a country more beautiful than the one we received from our fathers.

*

The Europeans' limited room for maneuver calls for greater lucidity, but no less determination. If they have to throw all their national and popular weight behind the EU, why is the latter worth anything? In the first place, because Europe cannot be made any other way, to expect a sudden upheaval or a providential catastrophe is to ignore the principle of continuity. Even "providence works in the woodwork," as Paul Morand put it. Europe will *not* be built on the edge of the grave. The quote belongs to Friedrich Nietzsche, who used it in a context that is foreign to us; today, it is the prerogative of those who wish to be prophets on the cheap. Europe will not spring from nothing: it is a rhetorical trick that invites us to find in the worst a germ of the best.

Secondly, there is no doubt about the Old Continent's weakening position in the world. Despite the cult of the economy, Europe produced 22% of the world's wealth in 2014, compared with 75% a century earlier. It is regaining the position assigned to it by its size, having spread to the four horizons the tools that had ensured its hegemony and now enrich others. Economic integration, designed to hinder the political renaissance of its component parts, must be viewed pragmatically. As a reality now independent of its original vocation. Europe began with the ECSC and the EEC in the smoldering ruins of war. It continued as a single market when the West was drifting on the sea of oil at the end of history. Now, the storm is roaring in a world where the downfall of nations is due to other phenomena, notably nurtured within them. Time is necessary for

---

[135] The EU's management of the pandemic was exemplary in this respect: first of all, it shone through its nullity – in the sense of absence or even inanity – instead of itself forming a border with the rest of the world. Then, the mechanisms for reviving the economy consisted of amalgamating the potential of each member state, in order to conceal the failings of the whole, instead of offering support to each country by means of cohesion in the face of the outside world.

everything, especially under the tyranny of immediacy and at a time when the economy polarizes international relations. For decades, administrative law has been a barrier to public power in the EU: a tool in the still inert hand of political will.

The European Union inspires neither sympathy nor loyalty. But some opposition has less to do with national patriotism than with systematic and sterile detestation. It is the symmetrical counterpart of the unhealthy jealousy many Eurocrats feel towards nations older and more prestigious than their glass-and-steel promontory. There are so many base instincts to overcome to prevent an obsession with dismantling from overtaking the creative force.

The economy or the burden of contemporary man

These considerations force us to turn our gaze towards the abyss of European economic antagonisms. The invisible hand is sowing discord. Brexit seemed like a divorce between two spouses gnawed by avarice and still plagued by unsettled issues. At a time of new ruptures, this economic war in Europe indicates where the peril grows, but also what saves. As nothing springs from nothing, our reflection is once again rooted in illiberal Hungary.

We have already mentioned[136] the heterodox economic policy implemented by Fidesz from 2010 onwards, in view of the international hostility it prompted.[137] The country's recovery requires renewed strength, which can only be drawn from the people themselves. In 2017, the Prime Minister detailed in Tusványos the ten points that characterize a sovereign country:

> First of all, a strong nation and a strong state does not live on other people's money. The nation's recovery begins with putting it back to work: Of the 10 million Hungarians [in 2009], 3.6 million were working, of whom 1.8 million paid taxes. They were the ones carrying the country's burdens on their backs. Clearly, this was a

---

[136] see Chapter V.
[137] A detailed analysis of the relationship between the Central European economy and the EU can be found on the Visegrad Post: https://visegradpost.com/fr/ 2018/03/13/leurope-centrale-et-leconomie-europeenne/

long and painful form of suicide. Incidentally, today 4.5 million Hungarians are in work, and everyone pays taxes.[138]

Viktor Orbán treats the economy as a tool in the service of a policy: that of national power. Economic growth in Hungary is more than the acceleration of elementary particles under the reign of merchandise. It is a dimension of reality to which politics defies, the better to direct it according to its sovereign will.[139] At least the illiberal effort tends to establish and maintain this hierarchy. The Central European economy is characterized first and foremost by low labor costs compared to the European average. This structural poverty is causing emigration that is detrimental to the entire region. To remedy this situation, Hungary is working hard to build up an industrial base as a source of sustainable wealth. While foreign investment is certainly a factor, the country is increasingly relying on its own capital. This is the strategic role that the State assigns to the European Structural Funds: a way of offsetting the capital income taken from the wealth produced in Hungary by a rentier minority in the West.[140]

The integration of Central Europe into the EU in 2004 established political isonomy between "economic partners" that are, in fact, very unequal. The advantage of the weak over the strong – the attractiveness of cheap labor – has led to the phenomenon of relocation from west to east. Some Western observers denounce this biased competition: the gains of the East come from the losses of the West. This aspect of the question is important because it is a factor not only of discord between governments, but also of resentment between peoples. First of all, the East-West cross-

---

[138] Viktor Orbán, July 27, 2019, Tusványos speech.

[139] For only conscience can be sovereign, and economics has none of that. The following reflection further illustrates the extent to which concern for national continuity outweighs short-term economic interest in Hungarian thought. "I also think that there are desperate situations where shipwrecked people can't take it anymore and start drinking seawater: it's also water, after all, except that it doesn't quench the thirst and only increases the evil. Those who claim to have migrants solve their economic problems find themselves in much the same situation." Viktor Orbán, July 29, 2017, Tusványos speech.

[140] Indeed, the hold of Western capital on Central Europe has lasted since 1990; several economists, including the Frenchman Thomas Piketty, have documented these cross-transfers:
https://www.lemonde.fr/blog/piketty/2018/01/16/2018-lannee-de-leurope/

fertilization is not symmetrical. Western capital collects rent when Eastern workers produce wealth. On the other hand, the Western worker loses out twice: he contributes to the structural funds through his taxes; and if he is a worker, he may have lost his job, exported elsewhere.

How can this blatant double punishment be remedied, and who should be incriminated? The Slav who has to work 40 hours a week for a monthly salary of 300 to 400 euros? Or the company that relocates to increase its margins? Or the Western state, a passive watchdog as its economy is dismantled? If we observe the decision-making chain activated in Central Europe, we can say that the people first imbue the elite with their aspirations, and then the state, committed to the general interest, imposes limits on economic players. The dysfunction therefore lies in the yawning gap between Western societies and their elites, which can only be corrected by a return to public power in the interests of the people. The difference lies between countries that introduce a national dimension to their political economy and those that abandon themselves unrestrictedly to the mobility of production factors.

Comparing Central Europe with the West reaches its limits here, as the single currency binds heterogeneous economies and paralyzes state politics. The Visegrád countries do not experience the determinisms of a declining power, still under the morphine of its residual wealth.

Western Europe itself is, to say the least, dual: Germanic Europe and Latin Europe. The former is, by and large, successsfully integrated into globalization. It finds in Central Europe a profitable workshop and a back-up market, and benefits from a weak euro. Broadly speaking, Latin Europe suffers from the comparative advantages of the North, without being able to remedy them, for lack of room to maneuver.

If changes are needed in Western Europe, they will come first in Latin Europe, as Rome has already shown. If Italy can maintain the same fortitude that Budapest has shown over the last 14 years, the recomposition of Europe would enter a new phase. Liberal logic reigns in Brussels just as much as states submit to it at home. Faced with the Carolingian metropolis, so hegemonic and disoriented at the same time, Latin and Central Europe can find common ground. Nations must reject the specialization of European economies under the pressure of a competition that is more alienating than stimulating. If Central Europe still exploits this to its advantage, the Latins must contain it in their own interests, unilaterally if necessary. Forced adjustment of the inappropriate European framework would create a new one, whereas the abolition of the European framework would not create any compromise. This distinction has far-reaching consequences. The purpose of politics, particularly in the economic sphere, is not to evade adversity, but to confront it. Conflict is inherent to life, more so than ever in today's economy. The political condition is to accept it, to measure it and to limit it. Liberal *laissez-faire*, by disdaining this obligation, does not reduce conflict, but rather makes it invisible, and places the burden on the weakest among us.

Many still fear protectionism because it would open a Pandora's box of retaliatory measures. The question remains political, even ethical. To fear more harm from other people's retaliation than good from what we can produce and build, is to place little esteem in our own work, and to rely on the outside world as if it were providence. It is morally reprehensible – and absurd – not to defend one's interests on the pretext that they have a price.

The prospect of economic recomposition across the continent can only be initiated by Latin Europe, since the current imbalances weigh mainly on its shoulders. It is by no means a foregone conclusion, since any change would have to be wrenched away from inevitability. To take this upward path is to assume what is happening in silence: struggle decides the course of events. In this locked-in situation, necessity forces us to play differently, according to heterodox rules inspired by national interest and in order to accommodate the Europe from which we cannot extricate ourselves. But such a virile recomposition is overshadowed by a looser option – and one that is complicit in the federalist project.

No one disputes the structural deficits of Southern Europe in the face of Germany's trade surplus. That said, the euro could be doomed unless Euroland is completely federalized. Such a headlong rush forward would lead to the economic specialization of the continent, turning Germany into a factory where millions of other Europeans. The fruits of their labor would then be transferred to their stricken homelands, in much the same way as deserted French departments survive on handouts from Paris. This policy dismisses nations; how can they care about people? In fact, it treats populations like cattle that need to be provided with sustenance to keep them laboring. The fruits of productivity spread in this way cover up problems and leave them to ferment, while the competition for the most mobile would continue mercilessly until the next crisis.

This pernicious development increased during the Covid-19 pandemic. Under the banner of the "great reset," international decision-makers, notably those assemble at the World Economic Forum, are working towards the triumph of a globalized economy independent of workers, peoples, and states.

This is the common grave promised to decomposed peoples. The fall is gradual, but so is the recovery. It is based on a conviction that is a faith: effort ennobles, duty is everywhere and first in the heart of every citizen and every family, then in the communities and trades, and finally in the state.

Illiberal emancipation by itself

The moment has come when recent history sheds retrospective light on the path Hungary has taken and offers a continental destiny to the national path revealed in adversity.

The dominant Western discourse has tainted the Hungarian Prime Minister's political thinking with suspicion. When it comes to getting to the heart of the matter, we need to get rid of preconceived ideas. The history of Central Europe and its political identity were discussed at length. Viktor Orbán's ideas come from there as naturally as a spring comes out of a mountain; it is a resurgence called forth by the century, a powerful movement that simply needs to be recognized and appropriated: it is a European destiny. This thinking is more patrimonial than national, to the extent that it cannot be linked to Hungary alone: we have decided to call it "Visegrád," even though Viktor Orbán is its instigator. The annual State of the Nation speeches, at Tusványos or on the occasion of national celebrations, offer abundant material. Insofar as the countries of Europe are brothers, descended from a common stock and civilization, the way in which Visegrád entered the new century should inspire the peoples of the West as they are reborn or fade away.

*

Fidesz is not only the Hungarian acronym for the Alliance of Young Democrats, it also recalls the Latin word *fides*: "fidelity." The most spiritual fidelity combines with the most prosaic pragmatism to produce a fruitful policy. Remedying necessity without forgetting ourselves: this is the course of action proposed by Visegrád, and above all it requires courage.

Viktor Orbán's first run-ins with Brussels showed that, in order to stand up to circumstances, you first have to oblige yourself:

> If we are to defeat adversity and its mercenaries, every Hungarian must first curb the instincts by which he compromises his own destiny. And he must first make these changes within himself. In this way, he will definitively side with honor, zeal, hard work and, consequently, the Fatherland. This is the only path to freedom and true liberation.[141]

Courage can drive action; even lucidity is only a form of intellectual courage. And if Hungary finds itself isolated on the continent, it is because its "elites" cannot find the courage to throw off the liberal straitjacket.[142] Visegrád is getting rid of it, not for the sake of publicity or scandal, but because it prevents us from serving the people. Fidesz therefore intends to move beyond liberalism as soon as it returns to power in 2010, in a clear-sighted and pragmatic manner:

> In 2010, we realized that the cultural identity of our community, of Hungary, was in full decay. We saw that the consciousness of belonging to the nation was disappearing. We found that our communities beyond our borders were under constant assimilative pressure, which they were unable to resist. And we found that the physical capacity to defend our sovereignty – the police and the

---

[141] National Day speech, March 15, 2012.

[142] "If you act like this, you're contravening Europe's new core values; to act like this is discriminating, hurtful and downright criminal. This Europe has made a spiritual straitjacket, and discarded the lessons of hundreds - if not thousands - of years of government. We must first free ourselves from this spiritual straitjacket, because it causes us not only spiritual problems, but political ones too." Speech in honor of the late German Chancellor Helmut Khol, June 16, 2018.

army – was sclerotic. By 2010, Hungary was being drained materially, spiritually and biologically. So the Prime Minister and the government had to answer the question of whether these Hungarian problems could be solved within the framework of liberal democracy? To this question, we have resolutely answered no.[143]

This realization led to the real revolution, reducing the liberal talisman to a museum piece. The result was the adoption by Hungarian representatives of the 2011 constitution, which provides a general framework for national recovery. Nothing now stands in the way of overcoming liberalism, right down to its anthropological foundations:

> What we're now trying to put in place, follows a different compass and declares - going back to a well-known truth - that the right definition of the relationship between two individuals is not to say that everyone has the right to do anything that doesn't infringe on the freedom of others, but that you mustn't do to others what you wouldn't want done to yourself. And even more: what you would like done to you, do also to others. It's a different basis.[144]

After the electoral plebiscite of April 2018, which renewed the Fidesz constitutional majority, Viktor Orbán broadened the perspective:

> I believe we have been given a mandate to build a new era ... The epoch is a particular, characterizing cultural environment. The epoch is an order of a spiritual nature, a kind of common atmosphere, perhaps also a world of common taste, a kind of mode of behavior. The order, the political regime, is generally given by political rules and decisions. The epoch is more than that. The era is more shaped by cultural currents, collective convictions and social customs. This is the task ahead of us: to install our political regime in a cultural epoch.[145]

---

[143] Viktor Orbán, July 27, 2019, Tusványos speech.
[144] Viktor Orbán, July 27, 2019, Tusványos speech.
[145] Viktor Orbán, July 28, 2018, Tusványos speech.

*

"The state cannot remain neutral when it comes to culture, and it cannot remain neutral when it comes to the family," Viktor Orbán summed up in his 2019 Tusványos speech. At the root of a culture are the families that perpetuate it and where it is inculcated. Hence the "pro-family" stance of renovated Hungary. The demographic winter is affecting the country like the rest of Europe. Between 2010 and 2018, the birth rate rose from 1.2 to 1.5 children per woman, an encouraging but insufficient trend. This is a delicate issue, precisely insofar as the family is considered an institution in its own right, independent of the state. Even with good intentions, meddling in families is tantamount to belittling them and infantilizing them. The Hungarian Prime Minister's tone was uncompromising:

> A country in demographic decline and – let's be clear – not even able to reproduce biologically may not deserve to exist. It disappears. The only communities left in the world are those capable of sustaining themselves at least on a biological level. Sadly, Hungary is not there yet. And we must also recognize that in demographic matters, and therefore in family policies, the hands of governments are tied: for no policy is able to determine whether or not there will be births in a community, whether there will be births in a family, and how many. Only women can decide. It will be according to women's will.[146]

The laws do not boost the birth rate, but rather help to create a framework in which families can flourish. Hungarian social conservatism rules out a totalitarian takeover of society, as in the communist era, and also rejects the liberal "*laissez-faire*" approach. It aims to return the State to a point of equilibrium, against the deleterious tendencies that compromise society by catering to the whims of the individual. The State returns to a congruent role: to enable, first and foremost, those who perpetuate society to live in dignity. "What can the government do? There's only one thing it can do: try to create a family-friendly

---

[146] Viktor Orbán, July 29, 2017, Tusványos speech.

environment,"[147] Viktor Orbán asserts, opening up the prospect of the forthcoming parliamentary elections. To protect families, which are both vulnerable and indispensable, the Hungarian state is taxing multinationals. The combined hostility of the European left and international liberalism must be judged in the light of this reality.

> In terms of figures, this means - based on last year's figures - that we take 272 billion forints [almost 900 million euros] from the banking sector, 120 billion forints [400 million euros] from the energy sector and 55 billion forints [180 million euros] from the telecommunications sector. That's almost 500 billion forints [1.6 billion euros] a year, which we redistribute in the form of 272 billion forints [900 million euros] in tax benefits to people who work while raising children, 74 billion forints [240 million euros] in free food for children and 5 billion forints [16 million euros] a year to finance vacations for poor children. We provide free school books (I can't give an exact figure, because it's constantly rising) and we spend 210 billion forints [680 million euros] on housing for parents bringing up their children. This is the demographic policy, the family policy I'm talking about. In fact, the resources needed to finance it did not exist ... We are taking part of the big profits to redistribute them to those who work while raising children and who are thus concerned about the nation's future.[148]

*

From this serene self-affirmation stems the distinction with others. Far from being a paranoid obsession, immigration only appears in the background because it calls into question the country's identity. The need for self-preservation arises naturally when there is something to preserve. It's not that there's a gulf between Western and Central Europe on this point. We cannot conceive of a people without an identity, but there are people in the West who are amnesiac, dismayed or alienated, and Central

---

[147] Viktor Orbán, July 29, 2017, Tusványos speech.
[148] Viktor Orbán, July 29, 2017, Tusványos speech.

Europe must awaken them if it is not to give in to their torpor. Free movement exposes every country to the consequences of other people's choices. What's more, any major cultural phenomenon on the continent spreads to the whole of Europe. Today, we're not talking about the Renaissance or the Enlightenment, but the extension to this side of the Atlantic of the multiculturalism inherent in the perpetual colony that is North America.

Hungarian inflexibility in the face of migratory pressure stems from this simple awareness of being a people:

> There is no cultural identity without a stable ethnic composition. To change the ethnic composition of a country is to change its cultural identity. A strong state can never afford to do this, especially if some global catastrophe forces it to do so.[149]

By asserting its right to historical continuity, Hungary has proclaimed its right to Europe. Necessity compels Viktor Orbán to break his country's isolation; European interest is then understood as an extension of national interest. Migrant quotas are the tip of a general drift. While this immediate peril must be neutralized, the need to ward off its springs leads Hungary to propagate its fundamental orientations to its neighbors. It was thus in an almost fortuitous domino effect that Central Europe became involved in reforming Europe. To prevail against the Carolingian metropolis would be illusory. After all, charity begins at home, and the first thing to do is to establish a consensus with its neighbors and make the region a sanctuary. This 5-point objective was announced in the summer of 2017:

> 1. Every country in Europe has the right to protect its Christian culture; it has the right to reject the ideology of multiculturalism;
> 2. Every country has the right to protect the traditional family model and to affirm that every child has the right to a father and a mother;
> 3. Each Central European country has the right to protect the markets and branches of its economy that it considers strategic;
> 4. Every country has the right to protect its borders and the right to reject immigration;

---

[149] Viktor Orbán, July 29, 2017, Tusványos speech.

5. Every European country has the right to be attached, in the most important matters, to the principle of 'one State, one vote', and this right cannot be circumvented within the European Union.[150]

The Hungarian approach is one of "he who loves me, follows me," the antithesis of Western messianic rhetoric. It doesn't bother to construct a theory in order to subject reality to it: theory depends on reality like a shadow depends on the stature of the man standing in front of the sun.

Central Europe is no more concerned with anticipating a rupture than it is with assuming it. Viktor Orbán's inductive, pragmatic approach warns him against aiming too high, but he's aiming just right. If the national framework structures Europe, then the European Commission, which usurps it, is the obvious target. On a continental scale, Hungary is therefore sticking to a minimalist objective: to defend the interstate framework, which on average is much more permeable to popular aspirations; to ward off the sterile unanimity that is facilitated by the surrender of sovereignty. This line remedies the most urgent problem. The Europe of Visegrád is proposing a model which it is not in a position to put into practice for the whole of Europe. But it is up to the major countries of the West to rediscover for themselves the principles and pragmatism for which they have lost the initiative. Viktor Orbán does not accuse any nation, not even the Commission as such. He invites us to rid ourselves of an ideological infection alien to Europe:

> If we are now talking about the future of Europe, we must first affirm that if we want Europe to live, if we want Europe to remain for Europeans, the European Union must first regain its sovereignty in the face of the Soros empire. Until it does, there's no chance of Europe remaining for Europeans. Once the European Union has thus regained its sovereignty, it will have to be refounded.[151]

Indeed, it is worth concluding on this point: the consistent defense of nations in Europe means defending Europe's sovereignty in the face of all that is foreign to it.

---

[150] Viktor Orbán, July 29, 2017, Tusványos speech.
[151] Viktor Orbán, July 29, 2017, Tusványos speech.

Conclusion

Fidesz's roots in the Kingdom of St. Stephen are long-lasting. But the overall grip of the economy exceeds the forces of illiberal Hungary and other nations alike. The economic upturn is not a whitewash; you only have to stroll through the center of Budapest to see that the Hungarian capital has taken on the positive features and favorable look of a Western metropolis, or indeed better. Do we think differently than we live? A first answer was provided by the municipal elections of October 2019, when Budapest and other major cities in the country passed into the hands of opposition lists that tended to support the principles of an open society.

Europe is hampered by its mass, inertia and the ascendancy of material concerns; "de facto solidarity" plays an overwhelming role in the continent's progress: precisely that of hindering it. In these times, every consideration of a philosophical, historical, or cultural nature yields to the law of economics. The depressing apathy of post-political Europe is due to this spell, which both controls and hypnotizes it. Capital rules. Human genius is absorbed by innovation for the sake of competitiveness, trade wars rankle the world's powers, and anything else that retains authority is dragged along in its wake. Everyone is fighting on this battlefield, because economics is the path to power, and power, people imagine, the path to freedom. But the means are so colossal that they make us lose sight of the end. Or rather, the end, conditioned by so many means, is lost in them. This is the "system."

*

If the perestroika of the West is not quite coming, it is because liberalism is still expanding.[152] Despite the prevailing depression,

---

[152] It mutates according to its historical vectors. So perhaps it's not where it's meant to be. To the extent that liberalism accompanied France's industrialization for a time, and since the 1980s its de-industrialization.

secession is not a foregone conclusion: the system has more hold over the people than they have over it. From this point of view, people's subservience to the system that dismisses them is their responsibility. In other words, the deep-rooted aspiration of the people to endure is more likely to find a career in the liberal impasse than in the uncertainty of a new era.[153] Between the dissolving wear and tear of liberalism and the wear and tear of the people, it is a race against time.

Our era seems to be one big shipwreck, so big that we lose sight of it. An intuition widely shared, albeit internalized: material comfort keeps the conscience in the shadows. Europe is a woman sustained by her dowry money, under the authority of the elusive spouse who leads her astray and disappoints her. This occupation must end. At the end of history, Europe finds itself at its beginning: alone, empty, purged.

Joyfully defending what we are requires going on the offensive; affirming that the people existed before and will exist after the totalitarian economic age, even that, one day soon, the economy that rests on the shoulders of the people and burdens them will return to them. But a people must exist and know how to say "we." The "we" that the young Viktor Orbán uttered in 1989 on Heroes' Square, when he declared that it was the whole of young Hungary that lay in the coffins lined up at the foot of the stage. This "we," constitutionally formulated in the Basic Law adopted in 2011, proclaims the inalienable rights of the Hungarian nation in the face of the new century's migratory tide.

The link between Renaissance and identity consciousness is not lost on the Hungarian elite that surrounds Orbán, as Professor László Bogár eloquently demonstrates: "The whole thing revolves around identity. For the aim of this power of global domination is to strip individuals as well as larger and smaller collectivities – right down to national communities – of their identities, in order to dissolve them the diluted filth of multiculturalism, the only state in which they become harmless from the point of view of the system. Anyone who has a strong identity is dangerous

---

[153] "Capitalism is seen as an imperfect system, but ultimately the only one possible. The feeling spreads that there is no way out ... Social life is no longer experienced as anything other than inevitable. The (temporary) triumph of capitalism consists above all in appearing as something fatal" (Alain de Benoist).

because the very basis of human happiness is that I know who I am, and whatever trials and suffering I have to go through, I know why I am facing them. Therefore, I am someone. This is the only possible mode of existence, both for individuals and for the various human communities. This is what this invisible global system, which pretends not to exist, seeks to crush."[154]

*

Awareness of belonging is only complete when rooted in an awareness of essence and origin. This full and complete acceptance dismisses conservatism as a way of thinking in relation to progressivism. A conservatism that is a fellow traveler in the process of liberal disintegration merely smooths the edges and consolidates the step forward in decline. And peoples wither away as the forced march continues.

From a well-understood identity point of view, secession from the system is not a matter of an opinion to be endorsed, but of a collective consciousness to be reconnected with - and in which to commune. There are a thousand ways of doing this, and mine is one of them. As a child of the Midi, I first awakened my sensibility of France through literature. The precise memory of initiatory encounters has stayed with me: the style of Cardinal de Retz and Chateaubriand acted as a lightning revelation. Their language seemed to enhance my own, and conferred a new nobility on the Nîmes coastline I was traversing: belonging to the glorious land of France.

Not that my little country expected any dignity from on high: it had it of its own accord. But it continued in the bosom of the greater France, and found its place there, and I with it. Likewise, France excelled in Europe through the flowering of its own national genius. The spiritual aura came from below, nestled in the heart of men and places, but the taste for excellence and some verticality called this spark into the high reaches of history and civilization. This territorialized intuition of identity, but of an inspired territory, gave me an infinite taste for travel, and the curiosity to grasp what lies behind the Costière, the Cévennes, the Alps. The need to see and understand, the exhilaration of walking and meeting new people drew me to Burgundy, Brittany, Anjou, and Auvergne. I was intoxicated

---

[154] Laszlo Bogar, *Visegrad Post* interview, January 28, 2019.

by place names, feeling them under my feet as they echoed in my head. I felt affiliated with the land and the people, responsible for honoring and defending them like my field and my family.

I believe this is the sentiment we call patriotism. It is the noblest of all, because it lifts man out of the narrow confines of the individual; it both obliges and empowers him, providing him with a sense of duty and a space in which to exercise his freedom. In Viktor Orbán, the bold son of Felcsút, this sentiment nourished a lion's heart capable of carrying the Hungarian voice across the world and into the future. May this sensitivity be at work in the youth of all Europe.

Bibliography

Bauvois, Daniel, *Histoire de la Pologne*, Éditions du Seuil, 2010.

Delsol, Chantal, and Botos, Maté, *Les deux Europes*, Éditions du Sandre, 2007.

Delsol, Chantal, and Maslowski (eds.), Michel, *Histoire des idées politiques d'Europe centrale*, PUF, 1998.

de Villiers, Philippe, *J'ai tiré sur le fil du mensonge et tout est venu*, Fayard, 2019.

Fejtö, François, *Requiem pour un empire défunt*, Éditions Lieu Commun, 1988.

Gastineau, Max-Erwann, *Le nouveau procès de l'Est*, Éditions du Cerf, 2019.

Hogard, Jacques, *L'Europe est morte à Pristina*, Hugo-Doc, 2014.

Janke, Igor, *Napastnik. Opowieść o Viktorze Orbánie*, 2012. English version: *Forward! The story of Hungarian Prime Minister Viktor Orbán*, Aeramentum, 2015.

Jenő, Szűcs, *Les trois Europes*, L'Harmattan, 1985.

Juvin, Hervé, *Le renversement du monde*, Gallimard, 2010.

Kundera, Milan, *Un Occident kidnappé*, Gallimard, 1984.

Léger, Louis, *Histoire de l'Autriche-Hongrie*, 1879.

Le Maire, Bruno, *Le nouvel empire*, Gallimard, 2018.

Marès, Antoine, *Histoire des Tchèques et des Slovaques*, Perrin, 2005.

Michéa, Jean-Claude, *L'empire du moindre mal*, Climats, 2006.

Molnár, Miklós, *History of Hungary*, Hatier, 1996.

Noé, Jean-Baptiste, *La crise migratoire*, Bernard Giovanangeli Éditeur, 2015.

Plaquevent, Pierre-Antoine, *Soros and the Open Society*, Éditions Le retour aux sources, 2018.

Poinssot, Amélie, *Dans la tête de Viktor Orbán*, Actes Sud, 2018.

Index